Library of
Davidson College

CONCILIUM
Religion in the Eighties

CONCILIUM

Editorial Directors

Guiseppe Alberigo	Bologna	Italy
Gregory Baum	Toronto	Canada
Leonardo Boff	Petrópolis	Brazil
Antoine van den Boogaard	Nijmegen	The Netherlands
Paul Brand	Ankeveen	The Netherlands
Marie-Dominique Chenu O.P.	Paris	France
Yves Congar O.P.	Paris	France
Mariasusai Ohavamony S.J.	Rome	Italy
Christian Duquoc O.P.	Lyon	France
Virgil Elizondo	San Antonio, Texas	U.S.A.
Casiano Floristán	Madrid	Spain
Claude Geffré O.P.	Paris	France
Norbert Greinacher	Tübingen	West Germany
Gustavo Gutiérrez	Lima	Peru
Peter Huizing S.J.	Nijmegen	The Netherlands
Bas van Iersel S.M.M.	Nijmegen	The Netherlands
Jean-Pierre Jossua O.P.	Paris	France
Hans Küng	Tübingen	West Germany
René Laurentin	Paris	France
Luis Maldonado	Madrid	Spain
Johannes-Baptist Metz	Münster	West Germany
Dietmar Mieth	Düdingen	Switzerland
Jürgen Moltmann	Tübingen	West Germany
Roland Murphy O.Carm.	Durham, N.C.	U.S.A.
Jacques Pohier O.P.	Paris	France
David Power O.M.I.	Washington, D.C.	U.S.A.
Karl Rahner S.J.	Munich	West Germany
Jean Remy	Louvain-la-Neuve	Belgium
Luigi Sartori	Padua	Italy
Edward Schillebeeckx O.P.	Nijmegen	The Netherlands
Elisabeth Schüssler Fiorenza	Hyattsville, Md.	U.S.A.
David Tracy	Chicago	U.S.A.
Knut Walf	Nijmegen	The Netherlands
Anton Weiler	Nijmegen	The Netherlands
John Zizioulas	Glasgow	Great Britain

Lay Specialist Advisers

José Luis Aranguren	Madrid/Santa Barbara, Ca.	Spain/U.S.A.
Luciano Caglioti	Rome	Italy
August Wilhelm von Eiff	Bonn	West Germany
Paulo Freire	Geneva	Switzerland
Barbara Ward Jackson	London	Great Britain
Harald Weinrich	Munich	West Germany

Concilium 136 (6/1980: Project X)

WHAT IS RELIGION?
AN INQUIRY FOR
CHRISTIAN THEOLOGY

Edited by
Mircea Eliade
and
David Tracy

English Language Editor
Marcus Lefébure

T. & T. CLARK
Edinburgh

THE SEABURY PRESS
New York

Copyright © 1980, by Stichting Concilium, T. & T. Clark Ltd. and The Seabury Press Inc. All rights reserved. Nothing contained in this publication shall be multiplied and/or made public by means of print, photographic print, microfilm, or in any other manner without the previous written consent of the Stichting Concilium, Nijmegen (Holland), T. & T. Clark Ltd., Edinburgh (Scotland) and The Seabury Press Inc., New York (U.S.A.).

June 1980
T. & T. Clark Ltd., 36 George Street, Edinburgh EH2 2LQ
ISBN: 0 567 30016 1

The Seabury Press, 815 Second Avenue, New York, N.Y. 10017
ISBN: 0 8164 2278 8

Library of Congress Catalog Card No.: 80 50583

Printed in Scotland by William Blackwood & Sons Ltd., Edinburgh

Concilium: Monthly except July and August.
Subscriptions 1980: All countries (except U.S.A. and Canada) £23·00 postage and handling included; U.S.A. and Canada $54.00 postage and handling included. (Second class postage licence pending at New York, N.Y.) Subscription distribution in U.S. by Expediters of the Printed Word Ltd., 527 Madison Avenue, Suite 1217, New York, N.Y. 10022.

CONTENTS

Editorial
    DAVID TRACY (in consultation with Mircea Eliade)   vii

Part I
Questions for Christian Systematic Theology

Is Christianity a Religion?
    JOHN COBB   3

Christianity as Religion: True and Absolute? A Roman Catholic Perspective
    PAUL KNITTER   12

Part II
Definitions of Religion

Definitions of Religion in Sociology
    GREGORY BAUM   25

Part III
Pastoral Theology and Praxis

A Culture without Religion? The Case of France
    JACQUES AUDINET   35

The Theology of Liberation and the Place of 'Folk Religion'
    SEGUNDO GALILEA   40

North America: The Empirical Understanding of Religion and Theology
    MARTIN MARTY   46

The Christian Religion as Mystical and Political in Germany
   MATTHEW LAMB   52

Africa: The Understanding of Religion in African Christian
Theologies
   MALCOLM McVEIGH   57

Part IV
Bulletins

Philosophy of Religion
   ITALO MANCINI   63

Religion in Current Cultural Anthropology
   VICTOR TURNER   68

On the Definition of Religion in the History of Religions
   NATALE TERRIN   72

History of Religions: The Shape of an Art
   LAWRENCE SULLIVAN   78

Contributors   86

Editorial

OUR theme has major impact for the self-understanding of Christian thought and praxis in the contemporary pluralistic situation. The purpose of the issue may first be defined negatively: the editors are not concerned to provide another anthology of definitions of 'religion' in the several disciplines, including theology. Such anthologies are readily available in each relevant discipline.

Instead, the theme intends to focus on the question of the difference which an explicit or implicit understanding of religion makes for the self-understanding of Christian theology and praxis. This question often takes the form in Christian systematics of two more specific questions: Is Christianity a religion? and What is the proper self-understanding of Christianity in a religiously pluralistic world? The two systematic theological essays of the first section, address these two familiar questions of Christian systematics. The first essay, by the Protestant theologian, John Cobb, first recalls several important discussions in recent Christian theology and in history of religion. Cobb next develops a constructive proposal on Christianity as best understood as a 'way' rather than as either a 'religion' or a 'faith'. The second essay, by the Catholic theologian, Paul Knitter, first surveys some post-Vatican II Catholic theological understandings on Christianity as 'true religion' and the relationships between Christianity and the 'other religions'. Knitter then proposes a constructive theological proposal consisting of a radical theocentrism and an 'inclusive', not 'exclusive' understanding of Christianity as a religion related to the other religions. In this first section, therefore, the reader will have the opportunity both to recall some familiar systematic theological debates on Christianity's self-understanding as a 'religion' or a 'faith' and to consider two distinct (even conflictual) proposals for reformulating the question of Christian theological self-understanding in the context of the emerging global culture of religious pluralism.

The first section, therefore, is focused on the concerns of Christian systematic theology and its self-understanding. The second section intends to shift the focus to another major discipline (sociology of religion) as this discipline informs the Christian theological discussion. The focus remains on the issue of the implicit and explicit understandings of the 'religious phenomenon' and how those understandings relate to Christian theological self-understanding. The author is an expert in both theology and the sociology of religion. Professor Baum focuses upon the debate on 'functional and substantive' definitions of religion in sociology of religion from Weber and Durkheim to the present. After reviewing some of the major contributions to this debate, Baum reflects upon the theological implications of the sociological discussion for contemporary Christian thought and praxis.

Baum's theological reflections provide the transition as well to the next focus on the issue, viz. the focus on Pastoral Theology in section three. This section concentrates its attention upon the implicit or explicit understandings of religion in Christian thought and praxis in widely divergent cultural settings. In each article, the author addresses a major topic in a distinct cultural setting wherein the question 'What is religion?' plays a major role for Christian pastoral theology. Five distinct cultures are represented to indicate the divergent forms that the question of religion may take in different cultural situations: Jacques Audinet focuses upon the question of a 'religionless culture' in France; Segundo Galilea analyses the debate on 'popular religion' in the context of Latin American liberation theology; Matthew Lamb analyses the notion of a 'mystical-political' theology in contemporary Euro-American, especially German, political theologies; Martin Marty discusses the North American notions of 'civil religion', 'public religion' and empirical understandings of religion in the United States and Canada; Malcolm McVeigh analyses the understanding of religion in the final communique of the Pan-African Conference of Third World Theologians in Accra, Ghana, 17 November 1977.

In each instance of this third section, the author has chosen a major topic as a focus for understanding the notion 'religion' in a particular cultural setting. Each author, therefore, reviewed the discussion of religion in these theologies and indicated the contemporary theological implications for thought and praxis disclosed by the understanding of 'religion' implicitly or explicitly present in a particular cultural situation. Although neither the authors nor the editors attempted an exhaustive discussion of the issue in any culture, the kind of situational analysis represented in this third section indicates the importance of understanding how the notion 'religion' operates in a particular socio-cultural setting and thereby in a particular theology. Precisely such situational analysis highlights the need for heightening theological and pastoral consciousness on the different understandings of religion actually operative in particular cultures, particular theologies, and particular movements of praxis. The editors hope that these representative situational analyses of section three may serve to encourage other analyses (e.g., among Asian Christian theologies, feminist theologies, neo-conservative and liberal theologies in different cultural settings). By heightening the Christian theological consciousness on the need to understand religion in a context-dependent manner, the possibilities of both responsible pluralism in Christian theology and praxis and the possibilities of cross-cultural analysis will be enhanced.

The possibilities of such cross-cultural analysis of the religious phenomenon provide the major focus for the fourth and final section of the 'Bulletins'. Here the concentration is upon those disciplines that attempt cross-cultural analyses of 'religion'. The traditional 'conversation-partner' of theology, philosophy of religion, is represented by the article of Professor Italo Mancini. The more recent conversation-partners for theology in an inter-disciplinary study of the religious phenomenon are represented by the remaining three articles. Professor Victor Turner provides an analysis of current cultural anthropology and, by focusing on the subject of ritual as performative, shows the possibilities of such cross-cultural anthropological studies. The analyses of Natale Terrin and Lawrence Sullivan provide two distinct surveys of the *status quaestionis* on the understanding of religion in the major discipline devoted to such study in our period, history of religions. Because of the importance of this discipline for theological understandings of religion, the editors decided to provide two bulletin articles in the issue. The earlier article of Gregory Baum has already provided one analysis of the *status quaestionis* in social scientific studies of religion.

Hence, this issue of *Concilium* as a whole provides four foci for understanding the relevance of the general question 'What is religion?' for Christian self-understanding and praxis. The first focus for the general question (section one) concentrates on the systematic theological questions 'Is Christianity a religion?' and 'What is the relationship of Christianity to the other world religions from a contemporary Christian theological perspective?' The second focus for the general question 'What is religion?' (section two) concentrates on the implications for Christian theological self-understanding of the results of social-scientific research.

The third focus of the question is praxis-oriented in the sense of analyses of the context-dependent understandings of religion in different theologies and movements of praxis in divergent cultural situations. The fourth focus is intended to provide analyses of the *status quaestionis* on the understanding of religion in these three disciplines (cultural anthropology, philosophy of religion, and history of religions) that attempt cross-cultural analyses of the religious phenomenon. Since these disciplines are the major conversation-partners of contemporary Christian theology for an understanding of religion, the bulletins in this issue should provide an initial focus for the necessary further conversation.

It is important to recall that the present issue does not attempt an exhaustive analysis of the complex question 'What is religion?' Rather, the more limited aim of this issue is to provide four foci where the relevance and importance of that question (in its various formulations) for Christian thought and praxis becomes clear. It is also clear that no clear consensus on the nature of religion emerges from these studies. What does emerge, however, is a clear vision of the importance of heightening Christian theological consciousness on these issues as well as an analysis of some major contemporary ways by means of which the question of religion is focused for Christian thought and praxis in both context-dependent and cross-cultural manners.

The need for responsible pluralism in Christian theology in an emerging global culture has rarely seemed clearer than in our own situation. Some of the possibilities for that responsible pluralism are represented in this volume. Many other alternatives need similar examination, as the editors (and, we are sure, the authors) agree. It is our hope that the present volume may serve to help focus these issues on religion for Christian theological self-understanding so that the wider conversation which this issue merely initiates may find the encouragement it deserves.

As the member of the *Concilium* board responsible for this issue on 'Project X', I would like to express my personal thanks to Professor Mircea Eliade, who, in the midst of his many labours, agreed to serve as a guest editor for this issue. His unfailing advice and consultations on the issue have been invaluable. I might also note, as several articles herein testify, that his incomparable *oeuvra* on the subject of the religious phenomenon has been a great influence on Christian theology. Although Professor Eliade is not, of course, a theologian but a historian of religions, he has contributed indirectly in many ways by his extraordinary work on *homo religiosus* to the revitalisation of the question of religion for Christian theology. The editors of *Concilium* are grateful to him for that work and for his assistance in helping to plan and execute this volume as a guest editor.

DAVID TRACY (in consultation with Mircea Eliade)

PART I

Questions for Christian Systematic Theology

John Cobb

Is Christianity a Religion?

1. CHRISTIANITY AND RELIGION IN THE AMERICAN SCENE

TO THE proverbial man in the street in the English-speaking world the question, 'Is Christianity a religion?' still sounds silly. Of course Christianity is a religion! Not long ago, for many, Christianity *was* religion. 'Getting religion' was synonymous, at least in the American Bible belt, with Christian conversion. To say that a person was deeply religious was tantamount to saying that person was an earnest and active Christian believer.

The American university was not far removed from this man-in-the-street mentality. Nearly twenty-five years ago I was part of a committee planning to develop a Ph.D. programme in a graduate school. The faculty would be drawn largely from the theological school. The majority of the committee, sensitive to some of the issues which will be discussed below, proposed that we call the programme 'theological studies'. Opposition came from sociologists and psychologists of religion, who wished to use the more conventional term, 'religion', not because they intended to study the sociology or psychology of Muslims or Hindus, but because they feared that the term 'theological' implied a certain type of approach which was insufficiently secular! The graduate school supported the minority, assuming that the subject matter of the programme would be Christianity, but seeing no problem in this close identification of Christianity and religion.

Even today much that passes for philosophy of religion in the English-speaking world is a philosophical study of traditional Christian beliefs. This is especially true where the approach is that of ordinary-language philosophy. It is true that the focus is more on those beliefs that are shared with traditional Jews and Muslims than on those that are distinctively Christian. But there is remarkably little sensitivity to the differences present even here. It is assumed that 'other religions' must believe much the same things that Christians have traditionally believed.

Of course there are other styles of philosophy of religion, and even among the ordinary-language philosophers there are signs of change. The word 'religion' carries a certain weight. Departments of religion have felt it necessary to show that they are truly departments of *religion* by including the study of religions other than Christianity. Indeed the pressure in some cases has been to turn away from Christianity almost entirely! It is felt to be safer and somehow more academic to study Jainism or a traditional African religion than to study the Bible. In this context philosophers of religion are forced to pay attention to topics other than traditional Christian beliefs.

When the National Association of Biblical Instructors evolved into the American Academy of Religion the shifts in university emphasis combined with the pressure of the new terminology led to a greatly changed emphasis. Although the study of Christianity still plays a considerable role, Christian theology has almost disappeared.

The problem for theology in this new context is that its topic is not religion. Theology deals with God, the world, and humanity, and only incidentally with religion. If theology is to be studied under the rubric of religion it must be as an expression of religion. But that means that one studies such expressions of other people; one does not develop one's own theology.

The *Journal of the American Academy of Religion* shows sensitivity to this point. The Book Notices are organised as follows: religions of Western antiquity; Far Eastern religions; American religious history; religions in India; early modern Western religious studies; Judaica; Islamic studies; contemporary Christian thought; philosophy of religion; philosophy; ethics; psychology of religion; arts, literature, and religion; and comparative history of religions. Of the forty-five books reviewed in the most recent issue, March 1979, only two represent efforts of positive Christian theological statement. They are both Catholic.

2. THE THEOLOGICAL DEBATE

Section 1 has shown that identification of Christianity as a religion has had a pronounced sociological effect in American universities and scholarly associations. Christian theology is now largely restricted to theological seminaries. Here, too, in the continuing work of theology, it is important whether Christianity is viewed as a religion. When it is, it appears as the articulation and clarification of particular religious beliefs. This requires of the theologian an understanding of what religious beliefs are in general and then a determination of what is particular to the Christian religion. Thus religion as such or in general becomes the context of Christian theology. The pressure exerted by this approach on Christian theology was keenly appreciated by Karl Barth. He is the first to have declared effectively that Christianity is *not* a religion.

This declaration was against the background of German nineteenth-century theology. Hegel, Schleiermacher, Troeltsch, and Rudolf Otto were among the impressive company of those who believed that Christianity *was* a religion, that this was theologically important, and that the task of theology was to show the supreme place of Christianity among the religions. To do so, German scholars saw that they needed to establish the essence of religion as such and then to show how the norms involved in that essence are most perfectly fulfilled in Christianity. The essence of religion would be, then, some aspect or category of universal human experience, and the religions would be ways in which human beings expressed that feature of their experience.

Barth rightly saw that this approach to Christian theology profoundly altered its character. One no longer attended to the Bible to hear what God had to say. One studied the Bible as an expression of religious experience which could be compared with other such expressions. At its heart there could be no difference between the religious experience involved here and elsewhere. One could not speak of anything God did or said. One could only speak of human experiences which expressed themselves in language about what God did or said. To view Christianity as a religion was to view it as human experience and activity. Against this, Barth insisted that Christian faith is not based on a religious *a priori* or universal. It is a witness to what God has done in Jesus Christ. Barth recognised that there have been religious experiences in Christianity, but he insisted that to confuse them with Christian faith is a serious distortion. Christianity is against religions because religions suppose that they can offer people a way to salvation.

The Christian proclamation is that salvation is a gift of God in Christ. Religion is irrelevant.

Barth's condemnation of religion and insistence on a totally different horizon for the interpretation of Christianity was a healthy corrective from which we still have much to learn. Unfortunately, it had some negative effects as well. First, it divorced the study of theology from the study of the history of religions, so that these two disciplines have proceeded in the past half century with little mutual influence. To insist on Christian distinctiveness is one thing. For Christian theologians to be ignorant of the great traditions of the East is quite another! Second, Barth's condemnation led theologians to false views of Eastern traditions. Theologians assumed that the category of religion which they now denied to Christianity applied to all the other great traditions, whereas in fact none of them are well served by being interpreted primarily in this horizon. Third, it encouraged a new fideism and supernaturalism. The Christian witness to Jesus Christ was cut off from any form of evidence, historical explanation, or philosophical grounding. One simply called for the arbitrary act of belief, or rather one supposed that the Holy Spirit worked the miracle of humanly ungrounded belief independently of the human context. Barthianism, for which Barth is only partly responsible, became increasingly incredible as the study of religion and religions advanced on all sides. Unfortunately, with its demise, theology as such has gone into eclipse.

Although the careful study of the various traditions renders the radical juxtaposition of Christian faith over against all religions impossible, it does not destroy the judgement that there are distinctive characteristics of Christianity. Without any suggestion of supernaturalism Franz Overbeck raised the question of whether Christianity might best be regarded as a systematic negation of religion. He could not bring himself to assert this, but he was impressed by the tendencies in Christianity to affirm the world as over against the tendencies of other traditions to deny it in favour of a truer reality. He withheld the judgement that Christianity negated religion on the grounds of this deep conviction that Christianity, too, at its heart was world-denying. But other theologians have judged differently, and a tradition of secular theology did emerge which saw Christianity as overcoming religious otherworldliness. Mircea Eliade contributed to this theological direction by his careful analysis of archaic religion and his picture of the contrast to it of the history-oriented prophetic-Christian tradition. Reinhold Niebuhr set this prophetic-Christian tradition alongside the many other ways in which thinkers have tried to find meaning in history, arguing for the superior insights of Christianity. Dietrich Bonhoeffer supported this tendency by his call for a non-religious interpretation of Christianity. Political theology asks us to understand the meaning of the gospel in terms of concrete acts of world-transformation.

Although there are differences in what is heard in the word 'religion' by various representatives of this trend, and although by no means all would strictly deny that Christianity is a religion, it is clear that they, like the Barthians, reject religion as the primary context for the study of Christianity. For many of them 'secular' movements such as positivism, humanism, and Marxism are the preferred dialogue partners.

While Christianity, or at least Protestant theology, has increasingly emphasised secularity, religious hungers have not subsided in the culture. In the United States quite religious forms of Asian traditions have won many followers, and new religious forms of popular Christianity have risen to compete with them. The question of whether Christianity is a religion is forced on the attention of theologians in a new way, and the nineteenth-century effort to understand Christianity as a religion has regained the attention of theologians. This programme was continued in a mystical tradition through the intervening years. Today the writings of Aldous Huxley, Frithjof Schuon, and Houston Smith are commanding interest.

These writers see a mystical element at the heart of all the great traditions. Schuon distinguishes an esoteric religion, bound up with the deepest mystical experience and the same everywhere, from an esoteric religion, which assumes highly diverse forms in different cultures. This mysticism cannot be condemned as simply a means of self-salvation, for the esoteric tradition knows the meaning of grace. To understand Christianity as a religion in this sense is to see that it has a much deeper response to human needs and hopes than its secular expositors have communicated.

However, to view Christianity in this way is to relativise all that is distinctive about it. Christian theology has no other function than to recover what is common to Christianity and to all other religious traditions. Indeed, if this is correct, then the time has come to declare ourselves committed to mystical religion as such, instead of to any one of its particular expressions such as Christianity. The consequences of viewing Christianity as a religion in this sense are drastic.

The proponents of this kind of mysticism can rightly show that there has been a mystical tradition within Christianity. But when they point to mystical experiences and teachings that closely resemble those that are found in other religions, the historian usually finds that the roots are more in neo-platonism than in the Bible. That does not imply that Christians should reject a mysticism that is found in other traditions as well. But to regard such a mysticism as the inner essence of Christianity, when it is so largely alien to the Bible, is hardly possible.

These objections do not apply in the same way to such Christian mystics as Thomas Merton and William Johnston. In their personal explorations of Christian mysticism they find points of contact with other mystical traditions, but they remain aware that Christian experience is *sui generis*, just as each of the others is. Christian mystical experience, as they understand it, is richly informed by the Bible. To hold that a distinctive form of mystical experience is the essence of Christianity is far more acceptable than to seek a mystical *a priori* that relativises everything that is distinctive about each tradition.

Nevertheless, the objections to the mystical interpretation are not entirely removed. However important the interior life may be, it is not clear that the Bible witnesses to its primacy. Jesus' message of The Kingdom of God is not most accurately understood in these terms.

Whereas most of the denials that Christianity is a religion have come from those who oppose seeing Christianity primarily in its similarity to archaic and Asian traditions, Wilfred Cantrell Smith has a quite different reason. He sees that to call Christianity a religion is often to solidify it as one set of beliefs, attitudes, and practices to be set alongside other such sets. This formulation leaves one immediately with the judgement of incompatability. If one set of beliefs is true, then others are false in so far as they differ. The adherents of a religion can accept a wide variety of non-religious beliefs, attitudes, and practices, but against competing religions they must maintain the stance of opposition.

In justification of Smith's concerns, one can cite the case of early Jesuit missions in China. The Jesuits wanted to indigenise Christianity there. They saw that Confucianism was inseparable from the best in Chinese culture. That suggested that Christianity should not be juxtaposed to Confucianism as an alternative but adapted to it. That would mean that one could become a Christian without repudiating Confucianism as a whole. But in the theological situation of that time such acceptance of Confucianism was not possible if Confucianism were regarded as a religion! Hence the Jesuits made the case that Confucianism was not a religion and gained permission from the Pope to baptise Confucianists. However, this raised an uproar of opposition among European Christians who believed that Confucianism *was* a religion, hence mutually exclusive in relation to Christianity. The enlightened policy was never put into effect, and there were few converts.

Smith also notes that when we speak of Christianity and other traditions as religions today, our relation to members of these traditions becomes that of representatives of one community over against another. It hardens our lines. Instead of dealing with living human beings in terms of their personal experiences and convictions, we deal with them as defenders of a system of beliefs, attitudes, and practices alien to our own. If we avoid this and simply share our faith, we find that we have much in common.

Smith's position is a remarkable one. Whereas Barth had juxtaposed faith to the religious *a priori*, Smith declares faith *to be* the religious *a priori*. His motivation seems to be in large part to overcome Christian prejudices against adherents of other traditions. But there is a danger in this procedure. When one sees faith as the essence of all traditions, one may have to come back a full circle to the view that our own tradition is normative for our understanding of others. It cannot be doubted that faith plays some role in all traditions. But what 'faith' means varies widely, and even more, its role and relative importance varies. In most Buddhist traditions, for example, it is left behind in the advanced stages. To insist in spite of this that it is in fact the heart of the matter for Buddhists, too, as Smith seems to do, may be a subtle form of neo-imperialism. We should let Buddhists tell us in their own words what is central for them. The answer is usually different from what Smith's emphasis on faith would lead us to believe.

3. RELIGIONS AND WAYS

If we take the position that 'religion' means a way of binding things together, then Christianity truly is, or can be, a religion. Rationalism, romanticism, Marxism, Fascism, scientism, nationalism, psychoanalysis, EST, and feminism can also be religions, as can Vedantism, Buddhism, Confucianism, Islam, and Judaism. But most people do not hear only this in 'religion'. They distinguish religion as a particular way of binding things together from other ways. In *God and the World* (pp. 104-106) I identified four elements in what the word actually suggests to most of us: concern with a world not given in ordinary sensory experience; a sense of absoluteness (or sacredness); cultic ceremony; and interest in psychic or spiritual states. I will not try here to explain what I mean by these. It is my judgement that all the movements I listed above are in some degree religious in some of these respects, but that the degree and respects vary greatly. For example, on the whole Buddhists are more religious that Marxists, yet the sense of absoluteness may be as strong among Marxists as among Buddhists. Indeed, some Buddhists engage in a sustained effort to overcome this sense of absoluteness, as is suggested in the famous Zen saying, 'If you meet the Buddha, kill him!' For some, the Buddhist goal can be understood as freeing human beings from religion. At any rate, being religious cannot be regarded as necessarily normative to Buddhism in such a way that the more religious Buddhists are, the better Buddhists they are. In view of our current recognition of Christianity's role in the secularisation of experience and society, the same must be said for Christians.

If all that were meant by declaring Christianity a religion was that it is religious, the declaration would be warranted. But in this sense all movements or traditions to which people adhere with seriousness of purpose are religious. Classifying them in this way would tell us very little about them. We would still have to ask whether 'a religion' in this sense was primarily political, cultural, philosophical, social, or religious! Only after answering that question could we proceed with our inquiry. It would seem wiser to limit the term 'religion' to those movements or traditions for which being religious is the most important matter. There are some forms of both Buddhism and Christianity which are religions in this sense. But there are other forms of Buddhism and Christianity which are not. In approaching Buddhism and Christianity one should avoid presupposing that the most religious forms are normative. Hence the classification of either Buddhism or Christianity as a religion is misleading. The classification suggests that we can best understand both by examining how they embody religiousness, whereas their secularising tendencies may in fact be equally, or more, important. In light of this, it seems better *not* to call Christianity a religion.

I have used the terms 'movements' and 'traditions' in the preceding paragraph. These are more neutral terms than 'religions'. I now suggest that those movements and traditions which propose to bind things together and thereby provide a way of personal and corporate life be called Ways. This leaves open the question of how religious they may be and of how central distinctively religious emphases may be to them. It also employs a term which is indigenous to many of them instead of imposing a Western category.

'Religion' is a common word in our vocabulary, and this word has shaped laws, institutions, and academic disciplines. Hence acceptance of the proposal that the word be demoted would have complex consequences. I have no immediate solutions for many of the resultant practical problems. But the problems with continuing the past use of the term are also acute. I have indicated what questionable effects the hegemony of 'religion' has had on American *academia* and in the history of theology. Also problems of self-definition are acute even in such disciplines as the history of religions. The assumption that Christianity is a religion still hinders the efforts of those who call for a secular Christianity or political theology. Discomfort with the word 'religions' leads many to substitute 'faiths', speaking of inter-faith dialogue and of persons of other faiths. But if we are to change our language away from 'religions' we need to consider carefully the limitations of 'faiths' as well. It is time to consider fresh proposals.

4. PLURALISM AND THE CHRISTIAN CLAIM

Now we can assert that Christianity is that Way which affirms that Jesus Christ is The Way. Of course Christianity as it concretely exists is only one Way among many ways, and this fact is a profound inner problem for Christian faith and theology. We have already noted some of the efforts to deal with this problem. We can summarise and briefly evaluate five unsatisfactory options.

(a) Rejection

Some affirm that, in spite of the obvious fact that many people find great meaning in other ways, they are all fundamentally wrong. The harshness of this judgement comports poorly with Christian love and humility.

(b) Identity

Some claim that behind the apparent diversity of ways what is important is truly the same. But no satisfactory formulation of the identity has been offered.

(c) Paths up the same mountain

Since the evidence is too strong against the identity of all ways, others argue that they are diverse ways to the same destination. The problem is that this seems false. The goals of unity with Brahman and of bringing justice to human society are not the same.

(*d*) *Relativism*

We can take the given pluralism of ways as indication that in fact there is no standard by which to evaluate their relative merits. They are all different and all to be respected equally. This sanctions even the most naïve and vicious proposals. It leads quickly to indifference to all ways.

(*e*) *Syncretism*

We can piece together from all the ways that we like best and establish a new way. However, in the process we are likely to lose much of what is most valuable in all. Our new religion will have no more depth than we are now prepared to give it, and that is not much.

As an alternative to these I propose the Way of creative transformation as The Way which is Christ. The emphasis here is that to follow this Way is not to commit ourselves to a fixed body of beliefs, attitudes, and actions. Christian faith is confidence in The Way even though we cannot discern where it is leading. It is readiness to expose the security of established patterns to new challenges. Strange beliefs, attitudes, and practices which have some appearance of truth and goodness are among the most important of these challenges. When we confront them we can try to retreat along the Way we have come to some point that is safer, but that is not faith. We can argue against them and try to show that their apparent truth and goodness is entirely false in so far as they differ from what we have already learned. But that does not express faith either. Alternatively, we can open ourselves to learn from them. If we are impressed by what we hear and depressed by the problems we have encountered in our own Way, we may convert to the other way, but that, too, shows a lack of faith. If in learning from others we simply add new information to old, leaving the old unchanged, that is still not faith, for The Way is always a binding together of the old and the new. But if we are genuinely open to the new, allowing it to transform the old, not destroying but fulfilling it, that is faith. This is the Way of creative tranformation.

This is the Way of healthy growth in personal life. It is also the Way the Church has followed at its best in meeting the challenges of history. The first great challenge was the encounter with the Platonic and Stoic ways. Some Christians avoided the challenge, and other simply rejected Greek wisdom. Still others, in their openness to the philosophers, abandoned the Christian Way altogether. But after much struggle, the Church as a whole integrated the wisdom of the greatest Greeks into its own life. That was not, could not have been, by simply adding Greek philosophy to biblical teaching. It involved a transformation of what had been believed along with its accompanying attitudes and actions. There were risks. In some respects what happened involved loss of what was valuable in the biblical heritage, and it took the new biblical studies initiated in the Renaissance to bring some of these elements to the fore again. Nevertheless, fundamentally, with all the imperfections of every historical movement, the Church's integration of Greek thought into its life was an act of faith. Christianity was creatively transformed. It followed The Way.

In our encounter with the traditional religious ways of Asia, the situation is similar. Here, too, we encounter an alien truth and goodness. Here, too, we are prone to turn back to a place on the Way that did not include this challenge or simply to reject everything in these traditions that is strange to our heritage. Once again, Christians weary of their Way are converting to Hindu and Buddhist ways. Others are simply adding meditative practices and other spiritual disciplines of the East to their Christian activities. But here, too, we have the opportunity to be creatively transformed. The risks are great, and there is no doubt that we are making and will continue to make mistakes.

But to refuse to be open to creative transformation would be faithlessly to leave The Way.

If we understand The Way which is Christ in this fashion, then we need not be disturbed that factually Christianity is one Way among others. That recognition no longer leads to relativism. If the ways simply lie alongside one another so that one must choose among them, and if there are no criteria by which to choose, then relativism results. But if the way which is Christ is The Way of being creatively transformed by all those other ways which have something of worth to teach us, then the way that is Christ can indeed be for us The Way. It is not for us to claim that Christianity is The Way which already possesses all truth and goodness. It is enough to affirm that Christ is The Way which is open to all truth and goodness. Our claim is not that we have arrived. It is that we are on The Way.

But our pluralistic conscience requires that we ask whether other ways cannot equally claim to be The Way. That question is not to be answered *a priori* either by a generous 'of course' or by insistence on Christian uniqueness. Every claimant requires honest and open examination. We cannot avoid our Christian biases in the process of such examination, and we should acknowledge them and discount our own judgements accordingly. But we should not blind ourselves thereby to what is great and distinctive in The Way that is Christ.

The Christian claim depends upon an eschatological orientation of the Christian way which distinguishes it from many other ways. Christian faith involves openness to the new, whereas religious ways that believe that the perfect is the primordial do not have the same reason to be open to other traditions for what is different in them. It seems that the eschatological can include the primordial in a sense in which the primordial cannot include the eschatological. On the other side, the non-traditional and less religious ways are almost always limited to something less than totality. The are defined by commitments which inevitably exclude as well as include.

Even if there are reasons to think that many other ways do not have the same potentiality to the The Way as does the Christian way, we are called to remain open. The Christian witness is not that no other way has the possibility of being The Way. It is enough to know that Christ is The Way.

Bibliography

Barth, Karl *Der Römerbrief* (Munich 1922).
Bonhoeffer, Dietrich *Widerstand und Ergebung: Briefe und Aufzeichnungen aus der Haft* (Munich 1951).
Eliade, Mircea *Le Mythe de l' eternal retour: archétypes et répétition* (Paris 1949).
Hegel, Georg *Vorlesungen über die Philosophie der Geschichte* ed. E. Gans (1837).
Hegel, Georg *Vorlesungen über die Philosophie der Religion* ed. P. Marheineke (1832).
Huxley, Aldous *The Perennial Philosophy* (New York and London 1945).
Johnston, William *The Still Point: Reflections on Zen and Christian Mysticism* (New York 1970).
Merton, Thomas 'Wisdom in Emptiness, a dialogue: D. T. Suzuki and Thomas Merton *New Directions* 17 (1961). Reprinted in Thomas Merton *Zen and the Birds of Appetite* (New York 1968).
Niebuhr, Reinhold *The Nature and Destiny of Man: A Christian Interpretation* (New York 1941, 1943).
Otto, Rudolf *Das Heilige* (1917).

Overbeck, Franz *Christentum und Kultur* (Darmstadt 1963).
Overbeck, Franz *Über die Christlichkeit unserer heutigen Theologie* (Darmstadt 1963).
Schleiermacher, Friedrich *Über Die Religion: Reden an die Gebildeten unter ihren Berächtern* (1978).
Schleiermacher, Friedrich *Der Christliche Glaube* (1821).
Schuon, Frithjhof *De l'unité transcendante des religions* (Paris 1948).
Smith, Huston *Forgotten Truth: The Primordial Tradition* (New York 1976).
Smith, Wilfred Cantwell *Faith and Belief* (Princeton 1979).
Smith, Wilfred Cantwell *The Meaning and End of Religion: a new approach to the religious traditions of mankind* (New York 1962, 1963).
Troeltsch, Ernst *Die Absolutheit des Christentums und die Religionsgeschichte:* Vortrag gehalten auf der Versammlung der Freunde der Christlichen Welt zu Mühlacker am 3. Oktober 1901. Erweitert und mit einem Vorwort versehen, 3rd ed. (Tubingen 1929).

Paul Knitter

Christianity as Religion: True and Absolute?
A Roman Catholic Perspective

WHETHER Christianity is a religion has been much more of a focal question for twentieth-century Protestant theolgians than for Roman Catholics. And yet, Catholic tradition and contemporary Catholic theologians have dealt with the question, even though only implicitly and usually as a corollary to other concerns; in fact, they have taken a quite unanimous position concerning whether and why Christianity is to be conceived as a religion. To trace this position explicitly and to evaluate it, as this article intends to do, will provide a helpful basis for assessing both strengths and weaknesses in the Catholic Church's present-day image and activity.

In agreement with prevalent Protestant views (especially as articulated by Barth and Bonhoeffer), this study understands religion as that complex of phenomena, permeated by symbol and expressed in creed-code-cult, which accompanies (*ante, in* and *post*) the experience of the Transcendent. We assume, therefore, the validity of the distinction between revelation and religion, between faith and cumulative tradition.

1. CHRISTIANITY A TRUE RELIGION

Roman Catholicism claims, clearly and persistently, that Christianity is and must be a religion. The systematic foundations for this claim have been elaborated especially by Karl Rahner, who can be considered the Catholic spokesman and counterpart to Karl Barth in the question of Christianity and religion. *A parte hominis*, Catholic theology considers the human being to be essentially a *sacramental being*. This means that the human manner of existing—before one's fellows and before one's God—is historical, social, and political. First, if *historicity* is constitutive of what it means to be human, it is also constitutive of grace and revelation; grace not only takes on historical form, it *is* history and can be itself only by being and unfolding as world, body, event, symbol. 'Life itself in the world then belongs to the very content of God's inner word to us.'[1]

Man as subject and as person is a historical being in such a way that he is historical precisely *as* a transcendent subject; his subjective essence of unlimited transcendentality is mediated historically . . . this self-interpretation of transcendental experience in history is essential and necessary. It belongs to the very constitution of transcendental experience, although these two elements are not simply the same thing in an identity which is given from the outset.²

This echoes Aquinas and a foundational theme in Catholic tradition: 'Whoever honours God must honour him through something determinate. . . .'³ Here Roman Catholic theology differs from the widespread neo-orthodox view and maintains that religion enters into revelation not simply because God decided to make use of it; in a sense, he had no choice; without religion revelation cannot 'arrive'.

To be historical means, more precisely, to be *social*. This is another central factor in Catholicism's insistence that Christianity must be a religion. Just as the person cannot know an appropriate selfhood without existing and interacting with other selves, so revelation-grace cannot be known, appropriated and lived outside of a religious society. Rahner believes that to make religion peripheral to religious experience is to adhere to the 'late bourgeois conception' of the human being prevalent from the eighteenth to the first half of the twentieth centuries. Contemporary anthropology, strongly influenced by Marxism, has reaffirmed the radically social-environmental quality of human existence.⁴

Historicity also means that men and women, even in relation to God, are *political* beings. As Trent insisted, while we are saved by grace alone, we are not saved without our cooperation and involvement (DS 1525, 1554, 1555). This implies that we are called upon to effect, with God, salvation—a salvation 'yet to come' but also 'now to be realised'. Catholicism views the human person, then, as cooperating with God to form history, making salvation concrete this-worldly reality. And to do this, one must give shape to and make use of religion. Again, religion is an essential ingredient to revelation and salvation.

A parte Dei, Catholic theology understands God to be a sacramental God. Here we have the revelational basis for the anthropology traced above. When persons experience themselves to be historical, social, political, this is not by chance or because of vainly projected needs, but because Ultimate Reality is historical, social, political. Rahner holds that 'basically and ultimately there are only two possibilities' for understanding religious experience. 'Either history itself of salvific significance, or salvation takes place only in a subjective and ultimately transcendental interiority, so that the rest of human life does not really have anything to do with it.'⁵ Christianity's choice is clear, for in both Testaments it witnesses a God of history, a God not only using history to reveal himself but a God giving shape to history, a God, ultimately, identifying himself with history. The Christian God, in the very essence of divinity, is an incarnational God. And this incarnational thrust of divinity is carried out in religion, so that religion or the Church enters into the very event of salvation. If God is a sacramental God, religion is unavoidable.

2. CHRISTIANITY AN ABSOLUTE RELIGION

The strong Roman Catholic affirmation that Christianity is a religion contains or leads to an almost equally vigorous claim that Christianity is an—or *the*—absolute religion. The word 'absoluteness', as used in theological discussion, is of rather recent vintage and owns a complicated-controverted history.⁶ Walter Kasper focuses its present-day content: 'Catholic theologians as a rule take the absoluteness of Christianity to mean that Christianity is not only *de facto* the noblest of all living religions but is God's one ultimate self-disclosure, completely valid for all men in whatever age they may be living, essentially definitive, never to be superseded'.⁷

In surveying the history of Catholic ecclesiology, one can note an evolution in the concept of Christianity-as-religion from what has been called an *exclusive* to an *inclusive* absoluteness.[8] Theologians offer various reasons why, even in our age of tolerance, such absolute claims, at least in their modified form, must continue to be made.

A parte hominis, Catholic theologians argue from an ontology of freedom and from a phenomenology of contemporary needs. Human freedom, confronted with a multiplicity of possible truths and choices, is possessed of an inner dynamism towards a decision of final and definitive value. This is why men and women of our age feel the painful relativity of historical relativism and of Troeltsch's dogma that the historical cannot mediate the Absolute. Humankind is led by a 'searching memory' and seeks to discover and affirm the definitive, historical presence of the Absolute. Rahner summarises the argument and draws the conclusion: '. . . in the concrete it is only possible to live, religiously speaking, in absolute affirmation, and . . . among all religions only Christianity has the courage seriously to make an absolute claim. . . .'[9]

A parte Dei, the argument for Christianity as the absolute religion proceeds with an expansion of the Christian claim that its God is a radically historical God—a God who not only pervades history but who has done something unique and absolute within it. It is this historical positing of the Absolute which answers humankind's 'searching memory'; it is an act which presents humans with an objective, authoritative Divine Other and thus enables them to overcome their 'hermeneutical suspicions' that faith is but a subjective projection; more so, it is an act which grounds a 'special salvation history' which is the definitive, unsurpassable statement of what God is up to in general salvation history.

Such assertions lead to the ultimate theological foundation-piece for Christianity's self-understanding as absolute religion: its understanding of incarnation in Jesus of Nazareth. Here, it is argued, we have the grand exception to Troeltsch's law that the finite historical cannot fully express the infinite Absolute; here the *Deus semper major* has taken 'a surprising turn'; in Jesus we have the *concretum universale*. Thus Christianity, as the continuation of this event, possesses the *criterion* for all other religious experience and is the *representation* and *completion* of all other religions. Possessed of and by the Absolute-become-History, it is the absolute religion.

3. CONSEQUENCES OF CHRISTIANITY AS TRUE AND ABSOLUTE RELIGION

The two-fold understanding of itself as *a true* and *the absolute* religion has very practical effects on Roman Catholicism's internal life and its external relations with the world. What follows is a brief indication of what seem to be the most significant of these consequences.

(a) Consequences Ad Intra

Catholicism's insistence that revelation/faith must be sacramental and therefore must be embodied in religion has received very positive affirmation from both academicians and pastors, Catholic and Protestant. Such insistence, they say, enables the faithful to live out what has been this century's rediscovery: that the human being is a symbol-making and a symbol-needing being, that ritual is integral to all aspects of human existence, that a religion without symbol and ritual is a bloodless enterprise. Also, the Catholic recognition of the credal and ethical components of religion enables believers to achieve a needed sense of belonging, a place to stand and act, a sense of identity and commitment necessary to interact, especially critically and prophetically, with the world around them.[10]

The consequences of the Catholicism's claim that Christianity is not only true but *absolute* religion have not been, it seems, as positive. Whatever may be the human need to posit a 'definitive and absolute' act of freedom, it can be argued that the *fundamental cause* if the disease and even open rebellion among Roman Catholics today can be traced to the absolute quality that educators and pastors have given to Church doctrine, ethics and even liturgical forms. One might call it a maturing of faith among Catholics, but it is quite apparent that today while they feel the need for *true* religion, they are 'turned off' by absolute religion. They are painfully aware of how absolute religion leads to: (i) an idolatry of authority and dogma, (ii) a ritual and ethical practice which becomes superstition, (iii) a morality which degenerates into legalism, even hypocrisy, (iv) a sense of identity which becomes 'false consciousness' and hubris towards outsiders.[11] Among today's Catholics there is a shift from ideology (or doctrinal absolutes) to values, from certainty to seeking, from observance of law to creativity, from mere membership to responsibility,[12] in other words from absolute religion to true religion. But because official Catholicism persists in its absolutist claims, there is a growing number of 'anonymous Christians' *within* the Church—people who identify with the truth and values of Christianity but cannot be part of its absolute claim. As John Shea has pointed out, during the past 15 years, many Catholics have come to realise that the only way to affirm their religion, authentically and maturely, is to go through a painful but liberating process of *disenchantment*, i.e., to realise and accept that while their Christian symbols, doctrines, moral codes, liturgical forms are true and reliable mediators of Mystery, they are not Mystery itself. 'Mystery, the transcendent meaning of which Christians call God, remains Mystery. No finite reality, either the person of Jesus or the Church, lays exclusive claim to it.'[13] A Protestant observer, in summary, might comment that it is the Catholic claim to be the absolute religion that has destroyed the distinction, for all practical purposes, between revelation and religion.

(b) Consequences Ad Extra

Here we will consider primarily consequences for Catholicism's relation to other religions. And again, it can be shown that the Catholic claim to be a *true* religion has formed a basis for the positive attitude towards other religions found in the well-known statements of Vatican II. While the Council affirmed 'elements of goodness and truth' in the religions, it did not explicitly say that they mediate salvation.[14] However, a growing number of Catholic theologians (including K. Rahner, H. R. Schlette, P. Schoonenberg, E. Schillebeeckx, B. Lonergan, H. Küng, R. Panikkar) develop the conciliar statements and argue that the religions must be seen as 'legitimate ways of salvation'.[15] The basic reason for this assertion is the *very same* as that for the claim that Christianity is a true religion. If Catholic tradition holds to the universal possibility of saving grace, it must expect that grace to be mediated through the religions. To postulate that grace is offered non-Christians through interior inspiration, or special guidance at one's first moral choice, or a special illumination at the moment of death is to indulge in 'arbitrary and improbable postulates'. To deny that persons can experience salvation in and through their religions 'would be understanding this event of salvation in a completely ahistorical and asocial way. But this contradicts in a fundamental way the historical and social character of Christianity itself, that is, its ecclesial character'.[16] If God's covenant with Noah is a covenant with the nations, then covenant by its very definition must be mediated through the religions.[17] The notable differences, then, between Catholic and Protestant views of other religions can be traced to their differing understanding of Christianity as true religion.

When the consequences of Catholicism's self-understanding as *absolute* religion are considered, this positive attitude towards other religions is 'toned down', even radically qualified. Because most of the theologians mentioned above hold to the absoluteness of Christianity (Panikkar, as we shall see, seems to be a notable exception), they go on to argue that the salvation mediated through these religions is in various ways deficient and incomplete, unable to distinguish between truth and debilitating error, not as existentially available as in Christianity, thus containing more questions than answers. And in describing how the world religions are therefore related to Christianity, these theologians present the religions as 'advent forms', 'previews' (*Vorentwürfe*), 'pathfinders' (*Wegbereiter*), carrying out a role similar to the Old Testament; or as Vatican II phrases it, the religions are a *praeparatio evangelica* in which the 'presence of God' is only 'secret', to be revealed in 'the fullness of religious life' found in Christianity. Thus the religions are valid only till the full arrival of Christianity; while some see the religions as submitting to a 'judgement' and 'crisis', others prefer to claim an *Aufhebung*, by which they reach a point of 'convergence' or 'synthesis' in Christianity.[18] Such attitudes ground the controversial concept of 'anonymous Christians'. More recently, Catholic theologians are abandoning such attempts to usher non-Christians in through the Church's back door; they no longer insist that the Church must mediate or constitute the salvation experienced outside her confines; yet in the encounter with other religions, they continue to demand that all religions must submit to the definitive normativity of Christ and Christianity.[19]

4. FUTURE DIRECTIONS: FROM ECCLESIOCENTRISM TO CHRISTOCENTRISM TO THEOCENTRISM

In light of the previous considerations, a question arises which troubles many Christians: In order to be a true religion *must* Christianity, in fidelity to its tradition, also understand itself as the absolute religion? Some will retort that this question carries the feeling of *déjà vu* and will lead to nothing but warmed-over liberal theology. Such a dismissal of the question is much too facile. Inadequate answers of the past (were they totally inadequate?) do not remove the problem. On the contrary! The present-day consequences *ad intra* and *ad extra*, of Catholicism's self-understanding as absolute religion indicate that the question presses more than ever.

It is especially in light of a world experiencing religious pluralism 'in a qualitatively new way' that many voice the necessity of revision in Christianity's self-image as absolute religion. Ours is a world in which religions know and encounter each other as never before, a world feeling the demands for new forms of unity-amid-diversity (on not only religious but cultural-political levels), a world whose cultural evolution has entered a stage of 'historical consciousness'. This world presents Christianity with a new *kairos*; and to respond to this *kairos* it must search for new ways of relating to other religions, which means new ways of understanding itself.[20] This is so especially in so far as this *kairos*, as Vatican II recognised, requires authentic dialogue among religions. However, missioner and missiologist H. Maurier speaks for many when he points to an irritating problem: 'If Christianity is the definitive truth, the absoluteness of God's revelation to mankind, it only remains for the other religions to convert to Christianity. . . . What we have, in fact, is a dialogue between the elephant and the mouse.'[21]

To confront such problems and the needed revision, Roman Catholic theology must complete the evolution in its self-understanding as religion which has begun during this century: from ecclesiocentrism to Christocentrism to theocentrism. It is an evolution which does not negate the core content of previous stages; in affirming theocentrism theologians can still affirm, in revised form, the universal significance of Church and Christ. Only by carrying through such an evolution can Christianity truly be a true religion.

(a) *From Ecclesiocentrism to Christocentrism*

There is a 'Copernican revolution' going on in Roman Catholic ecclesiology, and it must be boldly brought to fruition. This means that the implications of the common view that the Church is *not* to be identified with Kingdom or with Christ, must be drawn: none of the religious forms of Christianity—creeds, codes and cult—can be absolutised into one-and-only, unchanging statements of truth. But in this regard Catholic hierarchy and theologians have *not* been consistent; they have not exercised the same caution and reserve as the early Fathers did in elaborating the *communicatio idiomatum*; they have tended to identify the divine with the human. In affirming the divinity of its founder, the Church has become insensitive to the essential ambiguity of its hierarchical offices, its doctrinal and ethical teaching, its sacramental system, its life and practice, in short, its religion.[22] Such absolutising of religious forms is, as was pointed out, at the root of many Catholics' difficulties with the Church today.

The shift away from ecclesiocentrism also demands the clear recognition and proclamation that the Church is *not* universally necessary for salvation. The primary mission of the Church is not the 'salvation business' but the task of serving and promoting the Kingdom, by being Sign and Servant, wherever that Kingdom may be forming. This implies that it is not necessarily the 'Divine Plan' that, before the eschaton, all people must be members of the Church. Before the end, the many paths may well preserve their mission and necessary contributions. Mission theologians are drawing even more specific conclusions: 'The Church has the duty to be a sign and sacrament of salvation to the whole of mankind: it should help Buddhism progress along its own course of the history of salvation, and in a way work to make the Buddhist a better Buddhist.'[23] In this way there will be completed the shift from exclusive to inclusive absoluteness: from its focus point in Christ, the Church will include, by recognising and promoting, God's saving grace wherever it may be active.

(b) *From Christocentrism to Theocentrism*

For this to take place, a further movement must be made. The momentum towards a move from christocentrism to theocentrism was created already in Vatican II and in the theology which stands behind it. The Council shifted away from ecclesiocentrism in so far as it recognised that the saving grace and presence of the universal Christ was active beyond the Catholic Church. This shift was fostered especially by the ecumenical dialogue with other Christians and by the realisation that the Roman concept of Church was an obstacle to such dialogue. Today the wider ecumenical dialogue with other religions is forcing both theologians and Christians in general to recognise that it is not only the traditional concept of Church but *the understanding of Christ* that is impeding this dialogue. 'Even if we recognise that men are saved in and by their successive religions, but because Christ acts in these religions through his Spirit and in such a way that he ultimately remains the one saviour, we are still envisaging the other religions from within the absoluteness of Christianity; fundamentally the other religion is none the less disqualified. And, in every fibre of its being, it refuses to be disqualified.'[24] Today Catholic theologians are moving from an 'anonymous Christians phase' in their attitude towards other religions to a phase in which they being to question the Christological basis for Christianity's universal claims.[25] They are being forced to return to a new study of Scripture and tradition and ask what incarnation and the lordship of Jesus mean.

More precisely, this question inquires whether absoluteness, either exclusive or inclusive, is a necessary ingredient to the doctrine of incarnation and to traditional Christological claims. Such a question, made necessary by the *kairos* in which we live, becomes a new lens, a new heuristic by which to re-examine the Christological language of Scripture and the early councils. Briefly: it has been suggested that the absolutist qualifiers which undoubtedly are part of traditional Christological language do not necessarily form part of the fundamental content of what is being affirmed but may be a historically-culturally conditioned means necessary to make the fundamental assertion. What the early Christians—and Christians throughout the centuries—wished to proclaim for themselves and the world was that in Jesus we encounter the Christ; in him we are challenged by a full, a true, a reliable revelation of the saving God, a revelation which is relevant for all peoples of all times. And given the early Church's apocalyptic horizon, its fear of being submerged in the syncretistic religions of the time, its 'classicist consciousness', it was natural and necessary that the Church dress its proclamation with qualifiers such as 'one', 'only', 'final', 'no other name', 'only begotten'. But today such qualifiers may *not* be natural and necessary in order to proclaim meaningfully what God has done in Jesus of Nazareth.[26]

Some Catholic theologians are moving in this direction—beyond the usual understanding of the inclusive absoluteness of Jesus. They are, in general, exploring new possibilities in the traditional Logos Christology; they recognise that the totality of Jesus is the Christ, the cosmo-theandric principle, the universal revealing and saving presence of God; but the totality of the Christ is not Jesus and cannot be contained in and limited to him. Such a revised Christology would enable Christians to recover and reappropriate the underlying theocentrism found in the Nazarean's original proclamation of the Kingdom of God and still present in the message of those who made the proclaimer into the proclaimed. Even the Christocentrism of Paul was balanced by the reminder that 'You belong to Christ, and Christ belongs to God' (I Cor. 3:23). Nowhere in the New Testament, we are told, is Jesus simply identified with God.[27]

This move (or better, return) to a Christian theocentrism would in no way imply a downplaying of Jesus the Christ; on the contrary, it would demand an even more radical—and coherent—commitment to the uniqueness of Jesus. While it recognises that the universal *Deus semper major* can never be contained in any finite, particular form, it also recognises that the universal God cannot be truly encountered except in a particular form. There is an abiding, paradoxical tension between the universal and particular within all authentic religious experience. Christians can speak about the universal God active within all finite reality only because they have met this God in the particular Jesus. And it is the nature of such a revelatory experience that it possess an absolute quality: 'When it occurs it cannot but be decisive in its transformation of both self and the world by the God thereby disclosed; it cannot but be universal and definitive.'[28]

Yet it is an absoluteness which, while it demands total commitment, does not rule out the possibility of recognising other absolutes; it does not feel itself constrained to place Jesus in a unique or normative position in regard to other great figures of history and other ways of salvation. Total commitment to one's own particular Revealer is *not* exclusive of total openness to the universal God in other particular Revealers. Such an attitude is, it seems, a *conditio sine qua non* for authentic religion and authentic religious dialogue.

(c) A Unitive Pluralism of Religions

This movement towards theocentrism, preserving the relevance and necessity of Church and Christ as it does, still represents a radical revision in Christianity's self-identity as a religion. Simply, it means that in order to consider itself a true religion, Christianity does not have to view itself as the absolute religion. For many Christians this can be a threat to the validity of their faith; therefore in exploring the possibility of a move to theocentrism caution and pastoral sensitivity are called for. Up to our present age, Christian consciousness—Western consciousness in general—has equated the true with the absolute. Truth has been understood essentially as a matter of either-or. And it has been defined primarily by showing how the truth *excludes* all other alternatives, or how other alternatives are contained, even though anonymously, within it. The truth had to be absolutely certain; and that meant that it had to be exclusively or inclusively absolute.

No doubt we are dealing here with basic human needs for security. And yet, in a world of religious pluralism which is experiencing the value of other religions, in a world of historical consciousness which is recognising the processual, relational character of all reality, is not human consciousness being called to abandon its old securities and move to a new understanding of truth, including religious truth? A true religion will no longer be founded on the absolutely certain, final and unchangeable possession of Divine Truth but on an authentic experience of the Divine which gives one a secure place to stand and from which to carry on the frightening and fascinating journey, *with other religions*, into the inexhaustible fullness of Divine Truth. Such a true religion may consider itself absolute in so far as it calls for total personal commitment and claims universal relevance; but this absoluteness will not be defined as exclusive or inclusive but as *relational*. It will be an absoluteness which is demonstrated not by its ability to exclude or include others—but by its ability to relate to others, i.e., to teach and be taught by them, to include and be included by them.

At the present stage of humankind's evolution, then, Christianity and the other world religions are being called to join in a *unitive pluralism* of religions. While Christianity considers itself a true religion, it must recognise the possibility of other genuinely true religions. And this plurality of true religions can no longer exist unto themselves but must relate to each other, speak to and listen to each other in genuine dialogue. It will be a dialogue in which religions will not shrink from challenging and correcting each other; but the emphasis will be on their *need* of each other as they move, together, into a fuller understanding and living of the Mystery which 'is always present as nameless and indefinable, as something not at our disposal'.[29] It is a dialogue which invites the Church to engage in a truly *catholic* ecumenism.

While such an ecumenical dialogue among religions is still in its infancy, its first steps have been promising. It is enabling Christians to realise ever more clearly that every religious experience and all religious forms are, by their very nature, di-polar; Christianity's true revelation does not exhaust the Absolute and therefore must be related to and balanced by other, seemingly contrary, true revelations. As Wilfred Cantwell Smith has said: 'In all ultimate matters, truth lies not in an either-or but in a both-and.'[30] The Christian doctrine of the Trinity *needs* the Islamic insistence on divine Oneness; the impersonal Emptiness of Buddhism needs the Christian experience of the divine Thou; the Christian teaching on the distinction between the Ultimate and the finite needs the Hindu insight into the Non-Duality between Brahmann and Atman; the prophetic-praxis oriented content of the Judaeo-Christian tradition needs the Eastern stress on personal contemplation and 'acting without seeking the fruits of action'. Theologians such as R. Panikkar, W. Johnston, H. Dumoulin, J. Dunne, T. Merton have pointed out the rich possibilities of further, needed reinterpretations of traditional Christian doctrines/symbols which can come from such genuine dialogue with other true religions.[31]

Whether such dialogue amid a unitive pluralism of religions will lead to a still higher form of religious unity, and whether Jesus the Christ might prove to be the symbol *par excellence* for such unity—that is not known at this time. And it need not be known. What is needed is genuine dialogue. For the foreseeable future the task of elucidating Christianity's part in that dialogue, which demands a reclarification of its self-understanding as true and absolute religion, stands as one of the most urgent and challenging tasks confronting Christian theology.

Notes

1. E. Schillebeeckx *Christ the Sacrament of Encounter with God* (London 1963) p. 6.
2. K. Rahner *Foundations of Christian Faith* (New York 1978), pp. 145, 154; see pp. 40-41.
3. *Summa Theologica,* 1a-2a, Q. 103, a. 1.
4. Rahner *Foundations* pp. 323, 345.
5. Foundations p 345.
6. K. Lehmann 'Absolutheit des Christentums als philosophisches und theologisches Problem' *Absolutheit des Christentums* ed. W. Kasper (Freiburg 1977) pp. 13-38.
7. 'Absoluteness of Christianity' *Sacramentum Mundi* 1, 311.
8. An exclusive absolutism, which claims that to belong to the true religion and find salvation one must profess the doctrine, receive the sacraments, and accept the hierarchical-pontifical authority of the Catholic religion, characterises most of the official Catholic ecclesiology from the fourteenth to the twentieth centuries. It is blatantly present in Boniface VIII's *Unam Sanctam* (and supported in the treatises of James of Viterbo and Giles of Rome); Bellarmine's rearticulation of it in the Counter-Reformation became, as Congar observes, a kind of 'arsenal ... from which everyone drew' in Catholicism's struggles through the ensuing centuries with Gallicanism, different forms of state-ism, the Enlightenment and finally Modernism. Vatican I, with its definition of infallibility, confirmed hierarchical authority as exclusively absolute. (Congar *Handbuch theologischer Grundbegriffe* I [Munich 1962] pp. 808-809). Pius XII's insistence that the true Church is 'One, Holy, Catholic, Apostolic and Roman' and that all salvation is mediated only through this Church was adhered to by all the leading figures in Catholic ecclesiology during the first part of this century (E. Mersch, H. de Lubac, S. Tromp, C. Journet, K. Adam, M. Schmaus, K. Rahner). During this period, however, Catholicism's absoluteness becomes, somewhat confusingly, inclusive. Theologians recognise more and more the universal possibility of salvation but at the same time continue to insist on the Catholic religion's exclusive mediation of that salvation. 'Extra ecclesiam nulla sallus' becomes 'Sine ecclesia nulla salus'. Ingenious concepts were devised to include within the Church any trace of salvation outside of it: saved non-Christians belong to the 'soul' of the Church; they are 'attached', 'linked', 'related to' the Church; they are members 'imperfectly', 'tendentially', 'potentially'. (See M. Eminyan *The Theology of Salvation* [Boston 1960] pp. 167-181.) Vatican II did not remove the confusion. While it affirmed all the more resolutely the possibility of salvation outside the Church (*Lumen Gentium*, 16), it restated the necessity of the Church for all salvation (*Lumen Gentium,* 14; *Unitatis Redintegratio,* 3). Avoiding the complex question of membership, the Council affirmed that the Catholic religion includes all others as their perfection and fulfilment.
9. 'Christianity' *Sacramentum Mundi* 1, 302.
10. L. Gilkey *Catholicism Confronts Modernity* (New York 1974) pp. 17-23; J. B. Metz *Theology of the World* (New York 1971) pp. 115-116.
11. G. Baum *Religion and Alienation* (New York 1975) pp. 63-72.
12. P. Delooz 'How the Church Sees Itself Today' *Concilium* 67, 113-118.
13. *Stories of God* (Chicago 1978) pp. 32-36.
14. *Nostra Aetate,* 3; *Optatam Totius,* 16.
15. It should be pointed out that not all Catholic theologians move in this direction. What has been called 'the school of Daniélou' (it could also bear the name of von Balthasar) warns against excesses in interpreting the conciliar statements. Their general position is in basic agreement with the mainline Protestant (especially Lutheran) view of other religions: while they see the religions as bearers of a 'cosmic revelation', they stress that if the religions mediate salvation at all it is, especially in its understanding of God, radically aberrant. See J. Daniélou *Ly Mystère du salut des nations* (Paris 1948); H. U. von Balthasar 'Catholicism and the Religions' *Communio* 5 (1978) 6-14; J. Ratzinger 'Christianity and the World Religions' *One, Holy, Catholic, Apostolic* ed. H. Vorgrimler (New York 1968) pp. 207-236; E. Verastegui *Les Religions non-chrétiennes dans l'histoire du salut* (Unpublished dissertation, Gregorian University, Rome, 1968); P. Knitter

'European Protestant and Catholic Approaches to the World Religions: Complements and Contrasts' *Journal of Ecumenical Studies* 12 (1975) 13-28.

16. Rahner *Foundations* p. 315; see J. Heislbetz *Theologische Gründe der nichtchristlichen Religionen* (Freiburg 1967) pp. 70-101.

17. H. R. Schlette *Towards a Theology of Religions* (London 1966) pp. 71-74; G. Thils *Propos et problèmes de la théologie des religions non chrétiennes* (Paris 1966), pp. 69-79.

18. *Lumen Gentium* 16; *Ad Gentes* 9; *Nostra Aetate*, 2. K. Rahner 'Christianity and the Non-Christian Religions' *Theological Investigations* 5, 115-134; *idem*. 'Christentum' *LThK* 2, 1104-1105; A. Darlap 'Religion, Theological Synthesis' *Sacramentum Mundi* 5, 284-297; H. Küng *On Being a Christian* (New York 1976) pp. 110-116.

19. P. Schineller 'Christ and Church: A Spectrum of Views' *Theological Studies* 37 (1976) 555-559.

20. On historical consciousness, see L. Gilkey *Reaping the Whirlwind* (New York 1976) pp. 188-208. On the new *kairos*: W. Thompson 'The Risen Christ, Transcultural Consciousness, and the Encounter of the World Religions' *Theological Studies* 37 (1976) 381-409; P. Knitter 'Christianity and the World Religions: A New Era of Encounter and Growth' *Traditio-Krisis-Renovatio aus theologischer Sicht* ed. B. Jaspert and R. Mohr (Marburg 1976) pp. 501-512.

21. 'The Christian Theology of the Non-Christian Religions' *Lumen Vitae* 21 (1976) 59, see also 66-67.

22. G. Baum *Religion and Alienation* pp. 62-64; R. McBrien *Do We Need the Church?* (New York 1969) pp. 14-15, 112-113, 162-163.

23. M. Zago 'Evangelization in the Religious Situation of Asia *Concilium* 114, 74.

24. Maurier (note 21), p. 70.

25. Schineller *Christ and Church* p. 545.

26. P. Knitter 'World Religions and the Finality of Christ: A Critique of Hans Küng's *On Being a Christian*' *Horizons* 5 (1978) 153-156, 161-162.

27. R. Panikkar *Salvation in Christ: Concreteness and Universality* (Santa Barbara 1972, privately published); B. Vawter *This Man Jesus* (New York 1973) pp. 152-178; R. Brown *Jesus God and Man* (Milwaukee 1967) pp. 1-38; G. Baum 'Introduction' to R. Ruether *Faith and Fratricide* (New York 1974).

28. D. Tracy 'The Particularity and Universality of Christian Revelation' *Concilium* 113, 115.

29. Rahner *Foundations* p. 61.

30. *The Faith of Other Men* (New York 1972) p. 17.

31. R. Panikkar *The Trinity and the Religious Experience of Man* (New York 1973); W. Johnston *The Still Point* (New York 1970); H. Dumoulin *Christianity Meets Buddhism* (LaSalle IL 1974); J. Dunn *The Way of All the Earth* (New York 1972); T. Merton *Zen and the Birds of Appetite* (New York 1968).

PART II

Definitions of Religion

Gregory Baum

Definitions of Religion in Sociology

DEFINITIONS are to a certain extent arbitrary. They provide the social sciences with conceptual tools that enable them to answer certain questions and solve certain problems; but the same definitions may also prevent certain other questions from being asked and disguise aspects of the social reality that deserve attention. Sociologists argue about the usefulness and adequacy of definitions. What is culture? What is religion? What is work? Since definitions are formulated with certain questions in mind and certain ends in view, they reveal in one way or another what social scientists intend to do with their science and how they see the social reality to which they belong.

1. WEBER AND DURKHEIM

Some thinkers of the enlightenment studied religion only as remnant of a past age or sympton of alienation. Modern sociology took religion seriously. Max Weber and Emile Durkheim, the 'founders' of modern sociology, attached theoretical importance to the study of religion. Both sociologists made religion central to their theory of society. Since Weber always asked himself the question how society moved forward in time, he tended to focus on social change and studied religion as a factor of social change. He derived from religion the basic categories for understanding the transformation of society. Emile Durkheim, on the other hand, always asked himself the question 'How is society kept together' and thus concentrated on the social elements that produce cohesion and solidarity. He came to look upon religion as the essential factor of identity and integration.

Max Weber was so impressed by the enormous diversity of religious phenomena that he was unwilling to offer a definition of religion.[1] He simply followed the common usage. Religion was for him Christianity and the world religions as well as the primitive religions they had replaced, at least to a large extent. Only at the end of the most extensive research might it be possible to define what religion is. Weber was not as interested in the essence of religion as he was in its impact on society. Religion, he argued, provides the broad perspective in which people approach the world, their own activity, the earth to which they belong, the time that rules their lives, and their future, including death. Religion provides the matrix of meaning. Weber realised that this social function does not exhaust the meaning of religion, he appreciated that for the believing person religion has a trans-historical dimension, but he was mainly interested in the impact of religion on human life and society. As we shall see later, many sociologists drew their definition of religion simply from this social impact. Weber himself did not.

Weber studied above all the world religions. The claims of private religious experiences apart from a tradition did not interest him particularly. He had contempt for the faddish return to religion prevalent among the young generation of Germans after World War I.[2] Since these religious experiences were devoid of social impact, he spoke of them as religion *in pianissimo* and hardly recognised them as religion in the proper sense. He feared that some of these cults tried to revive the gods Christianity had laid to rest centuries earlier. For Weber religion in the proper sense touched the foundation of society.

At the same time Weber did not identify religion with the matrix of meaning it provided for society. He did not want to make religion a constitutive element of society. On the contrary, his intention was to show that the trend towards rationalisation, itself sparked and promoted (against itself) by Christianity, especially in its Protestant form, led in fact to the exclusion of religion from culture and society and created a wholly secular age. The matrix of meaning of modern society was not religious. Weber's decision to follow the common sense view of religion enabled him to defend the theory of secularisation which, we note, he lamented as a symptom of cultural decline. Weber himself was an agnostic, he called himself religiously unmusical (which is hard for his readers to believe), and he suspected that the great majority of people were in fact religiously ungifted. Even in the great religious civilisations, he thought, the vitality of religion depended on 'the virtuosi', the few religiously gifted people, who were admired by the masses whose own religion tended to be conformist, external and easily compromised.[3]

Emile Durkheim came to look upon religion quite differently. For him religion was essentially social. The beliefs and practices regarding the sacred united people as a single community with one heart and soul. In his younger days Durkheim argued, following earlier French social thinkers, that religion was a system of collective self-interpretation that played an essential role in traditional communities but had no place whatever in modern, enlightened society. Durkheim then hypothesised that in industrial society interdependence and solidarity were created by the complex division of labour. He later changed his mind. On the basis of his research in primitive and modern society, he came to the conclusion that symbols of world interpretation remain of abiding importance for society, even in the age of science and technology, and that these symbols are in fact both the power that keeps society together and the power that summons it to greater fidelity to its ideals. There is something eternal about religion.[4]

At the same time, there are no gods, no other world, no supernatural: Durkheim was an atheist. The sacred, the totally other, is simply society's projection of itself in human consciousness: it is society writ large.[5] It reveals man's dependence on the social matrix as a reality in consciousness that transcends the individual, demands solidarity, creates morality, and calls for sacrifice and even surrender. Even modern society, Durkheim believed, will eventually generate symbols of its collective self-understanding and produce religion. What the new gods will be like, the French sociologist did not claim to know. But he trusted that the utilitarian, individualistic, self-seeking outlook which dominated people's minds in modern society would eventually give way to religious devotion to the common good and to ethical norms appropriate to modern society, rational, democratic and socialist.

2. THE FUNCTIONAL DEFINITION OF RELIGION

Under the influence of Durkheim, sociologists developed what has been called the functional definition of religion. Religion is here defined in terms of its social role, namely to supply the matrix of meaning to society. Religion is here a system of world interpretation that articulates the self-understanding of the community and its place and task in the universe. Religion defines the perspective in which people see themselves and their relationship to society and nature. Not every value orientation nor every context of meaning is religious, of course; it is only 'the highest' or 'most general' symbolic framework that deserves this name. Religion is the symbol that provides a 'total' world interpretation, the myth that relates people to the 'ultimate' conditions of their existence.

The functional definition of religion situates religion at the very heart of society, in fact as a constitutive part. This has made the definition appealing to some religious thinkers. Religion is at the centre. Theologians have been attracted to the definition because it reassures them that religion is not losing ground and that theologians deal not with the marginal but with the essentially human. I cannot deny that I was enormously reassured at one point in my life by the attention paid to religion by some of the great sociologists.[6] Religion is a permanent dimension of reality: religion may change as society does, but it can never disappear.

This understanding of religion is not only attractive to religious people. Durkheim who first gave the theory its scientific formulation was an atheist. He used the theory in his arguments against French Catholics who despised the republic with its democratic and liberal ideals as an expression of moral decline, and remained attached to the *ancien régime* with its respect for religion and higher values. Durkheim argued that in the long run modern society will not be caught in individualism and utilitarianism, characteristic of the age of transition: eventually it will generate its own sense of the sacred, bring forth social solidarity and inspire devotion to abiding moral norms. The same definition of religion, we note, can be put to a variety of uses.

The functional definition of religion was influential among the sociologists who introduced Durkheim to North America. Famous is Talcott Parsons' interpretation of religion as the highest level of culture. Following his evolutionary understanding of society, Parsons tried to show that Christian values have increasingly been integrated into the secular symbols and structures of modern society.[7] Democratic society, society under the law, was in fact the creation of the Christian tradition. Against Max Weber who thought that Protestant Christianity had successfully promoted secularisation and prepared its own demise, Parsons argued that by a process of differentiation many Christian values had become part of the secular ethos and elements of the social order, setting free to flourish the specifically religious aspect of Christianity, namely the formation of the soul's relationship to God. As formation of conscience and consciousness, Christianity (joined by modern Judaism) continues to exercise the supreme cultural function in the creation of modern society. In this perspective, the American republic appears as the highest stage of the evolution of society and American denominational religion as the highest form of Christianity.

Robert Bellah also follows the functional definition of religion. He specifically mentions Paul Tillich's language of 'ultimate concern'.[8] If it is true that in the long run every person becomes ultimately concerned and hence in some sense religious, then sociologists have good reason to reject the theory of secularisation and look around for new manifestations of religion as the churches lose their symbolic power at this time. Bellah takes 'the new religions' seriously: he sees in them a cultural movement, in protest against the secular spirit of a business society and the dogmatic rigidity of the churches. The future lies in the creation of a more personal religion. At the same time,

Bellah also made an imaginative use of Rousseau's concept of 'civil religion'. He argued that it is impossible to gain a sociological understanding of American society without taking into consideration the celebration of America's national self-understanding, i.e., American civil religion, which directs people's thinking and acts as transcendent norm for the evaluation of American domestic policies and political involvement abroad.[9] This civil religion, we note, is not an idolatrous worship of the nation, it is rather a (Durkheimian) devotion to moral norms and national standards. Civil religion speaks of God, but it does not object if its adherents accept this divinity as a purely linguistic presence.

The functional definition of religion seems boundariless. No society can escape religion. It enables sociologists to designate as religion what people normally do not regard as religion at all. Religion can refer to symbols of national identity elevated to the highest plane or to systems of world interpretation, such as socialism or liberalism, that see themselves as wholly secular and define themselves against the Christian tradition. Religion here becomes universal. For some social thinkers, this reveals the nature of human existence. Not, as we mentioned above, for Max Weber! Other authors use this wide view of religion as an argument against socialism. Pointing to the messianic, eschatological elements of Marxism and the total commitment demanded by socialist organisations, they designate socialism as a religion and in this way discredit it as being based not on facts and science but on faith and make-belief.[10] Some social thinkers are willing to call religion all ideologies that lend themselves to the language of ultimacy, e.g., secularism, fascism, psychoanalysis. Such arguments sometimes appeal to Christian apologists. When people abandon the Christian religion, they become vulnerable to ideologies and to their own detriment assimilate them as substitute religions.[11]

The functional definition of religion has an affinity to Paul Tillich's notion of 'ultimate concern'. Parsons and Bellah willingly refer to this great theologian. We note, however, that Tillich uses the notion of 'ultimate concern', as sociologists do not, in a normative way. The only ultimate concern that is true and non-contradictory is God, or more correctly, since God has been tamed by language and institutions, God beyond God, so that every other ultimate concern is idolatrous. Among sociologists, the Christian thinker, Andrew Greeley, has made use of Tillich's normative concept.[12] All people are religious, Greeley argues, all have gods who sum up for them the ultimate concern in personal and social life. What counts from a Christian point of view is whether this divinity is in keeping with biblical revelation. The functional understanding of religion allows Greeley to explicate the meaning of God in earthly, finite terms, i.e., to specify the perspective on life God reveals and the kind of action this God summons forth. Coming from a Catholic tradition, Greeley is not willing (as Tillich is) to call idolatrous all forms of worship not in line with the gospel. Greeley is more patient in regard to the human religions which people endorse in varying degrees and which they often combine with their Christian faith. The struggle of the Christian is not an either/or choice but a steady growth, with moments of conversion, overcoming the ambiguity of religion in ever greater fidelity to the gospel.

The functional definition of religion is also attractive to secular thinkers who find it scientifically useful and illuminating. Why? Because it raises the question how the present order is symbolically legitimated, and reveals the hidden social function of science in the construction of society. Peter Berger, though no functionalist, often promotes this kind of thinking about religion, even though he has warned sociologists against the indiscriminate use of the functional definition of religion.[13] Thomas Luckmann, not heeding his colleague's advice, has rushed into the concept of 'invisible religion', designating the highest level of legitimation exercised in modern society by science and social scientific theory.[14] Luckmann argues that the churches no longer communicate religion since their symbol systems have lost the reference to universality.

Peter Berger himself occasionally follows the same line. The acceptance of religious pluralism, characteristic of modern society, prevents the single religions from being principles of world interpretations: since they are willing to recognise their partiality, they lose the power to define reality, cease to be religious and become akin to spiritual hobbies.[15]

But Peter Berger does not align himself with the functional definition of religion. For him religion has to do with a sacred reality beyond time. Religion is the sacred canopy stretched over the fragility and vulnerability of human existence, epitomised in death itself. With Heidegger, Berger sees in man's anxiety in the face of death and mortality the defining characteristic of human life.[16] The only force that call allay this anxiety is religion: only religion deals with immortal gods, the higher world, the transcendent realm. This is what sociologists call 'the substantive definition of religion'.

3. THE SUBSTANTIVE DEFINITION OF RELIGION

The sociologists who opt for the substantive definition clearly recognise the social impact of religion, but the essential characteristic of religion is for them the relation to the invisible world. This definition agrees more with the common usage of the term. This is a great advantage. The early anthropologists looked upon the religion they studied as the intercourse of people with gods, spirits and the supernatural. This approach easily led to an external view of religion. The substantive definition of religion discouraged some scholars from asking questions about the meaning of religion: They remained satisfied by a purely factual account. This approach easily made religion, all religion, appear as the realm of the incredible, the primitive, the unenlightened, the never-never land basically at odds with modern rationality. It also happens, of course, that functionalists, concentrating as they do on the social role of religion, neglect the meaning religion has for those who practise it. Weber never forgot that the understanding of religion remains incomplete unless one attended to its meaning for believers. Parsons himself, who has developed the functionalist approach, remarks that this approach easily leads one to forget that religion is not exhausted by the social dimension, that it has in fact a reference to the invisible world.[17] Whether the definition of religion is substantive or functional, sociologists only too easily overlook the meaning religion has for the believers.

The substantive definition of religion poses several problems. Does it really cover the world religions? It has been argued that Confucianism has no relation to the supernatural and that the purest form of Buddhism does not recognise a transcendent world. But if these religions are excluded, how useful is the definition? Durkheim invoked this difficulty when he opted for the functional definition of religion.[18] Does pantheism in any of its forms fall outside of the substantive definition? Pantheism teaches that there is a single reality, not two worlds. It can be argued, however, that pantheism recognises the world of appearances which deceives and the world of reality into which one has to be initiated, two worlds, in other words. The same argument can be made for panentheism, i.e., for religion that perceives the mystery of God immanent in the world or present to history. It also insists that there is a single reality, the world of history; but since divinity transcends the world in which it is incarnate, panentheistic religion acknowledges a divine reality in and through the present, the infinite in the finite, the beyond in the midst of life—and hence qualifies as religion substantively defined. Sociologists of religion with a Protestant cultural background find it often very difficult to relate this inner-worldly or incarnate transcendence to the religion of the Bible. Max Weber thought that biblical religion was exclusively 'ethical prophecy', i.e., a way of obedience to the word uttered by the God on high, and that one had to turn to the

Eastern religions to find examples of 'exemplary prophecy', i.e., a way of participation in a God-filled life.[19] Weber overlooked the mystical and sacramental aspects of Christianity. Peter Berger has the same blind spot in regard to the this-worldly or incarnate notion of divine transcendence: he thinks it cancels the biblical God.[20]

The substantive definition of religion is able to treat in its own way, often very convincingly, the wide range of phenomena dealt with by religion functionally defined. Sociologists speak of 'functional equivalents' of religion: by this they refer to the secular ideologies that demand a total commitment and mediate a complete world picture. They also speak of 'surrogate religion', referring to ecstatic experiences and ritual action not associated with a religion properly so-called.

The preceding pages demonstrate that it would be quite wrong to suppose that sociologists who define religion in one way share a common view, and those who define religion in the other way are united by a common perspective. In each definition several perspectives are possible. It does not make sense, therefore, to ask which of the two definitions of religion is more illuminating from the theological point of view. Both definitions can be used well, and both can be used badly. Some sociologists who stress the functional definition assimilate religion to other ideologies, neglect the moment of transcendence, and overlook the meaning of religion, while other sociologists who stress the substantive definition assimilate religion to mythologies and fairy tales and present it as a realm for the credulous. For the theologian the critical issue is not which definition of religion is being used but whether the treatment of religion is reductionist. There is a 'positivist reductionism', which wholly represses the question of meaning. Religion is here studied simply from the outside. Neither Weber nor Durkheim ever followed this way. The great sociologists always argued against positivistic reductionism. They took religious experience seriously, they were interested in the meaning of religion for the believer and its role in society.

There is a second level of reductionism, 'metaphysical reductionism', which presupposes that religion is a purely finite reality and nothing else. Sociologists like Peter Berger argue that in this sense all of sociology must be reductionist. Sociologists must suspend the judgement whether there is a metaphysical reality implicit in the religious phenomena they study. He speaks here of 'methodological atheism'.[21] This viewpoint fits well into Berger's position on the value-free nature of sociology in general. Berger is not very sensitive to the manner in which the scholar's world perspective or value orientation affects his research, the choice and reading of the data, the conceptualisation of ideas and the logic used to arrive at conclusions. The better position, it seems to me, is taken by Robert Bellah who argues that a metaphysical negation affects the sociologist in his or her investigation of religion. Unless he is open to a metaphysical reality—he need not be committed to it—he lacks the sensitivity to read correctly and profoundly the religious phenomenon.[22] Even Weber's work and more especially Durkheim's suffered from this. Can a wholly unmusical scholar produce a significant study of music? Unless the sociologist recognises that religious consciousness is not necessarily illusory, his or her instruments of observation and interpretation remain inadequately tuned. Bellah demands that the sociologist of religion recognise the symbolic nature of religion and be open to a possible metaphysical foundation: he calls this approach 'symbolic realism'.

4. MARXISM AND RELIGION

The question can be asked whether Marxism operates with a substantive or functional definition of religion. Marx was certainly exclusively concerned with the social impact of religion. As Durkheim after him, Marx regarded religion as the self-projection of society into human consciousness, but while Durkheim tried to show that religion embodied the best and the highest in society and hence served the well-being of the whole community, Marx believed that religion was a symptom of alienation, a symbolic legitimation of the ruling class, and a consolation of other-worldly hope offered to the poor. In a single remark, Marx recognised that religion can also be an expression of social protest. But neither Marx nor subsequent Marxists used the wider notion of religion to analyse symbol systems of self-understanding. Only Antonio Gramsci, who focused on the cultural dimension of the social revolution, tried to clarify the role of Marxist ideology among the people by calling it 'religio'.[23] Marx and Marxists used the substantive definition of religion, linking it inextricably to the other world, and for this reason remained on the whole quite insensitive to the role of symbols in personal and social self-understanding. A grain of positivism prevented Marxists from reflecting on the symbols in which they themselves perceived the world and on the commitment out of which they acted in it. The question whether Marxists defined religion in substantive or functionalist terms does not lead to much light. The more important question in regard to Marxism and religion has to do with reductionism.

It is usually argued that in his historical writings, Marx showed no trace of economic determinism and understood the relation between base and superstructure as creative interaction. Beginning with Engels, Marxist thinkers tended to replace Marx's dialectical approach by a mechanistic theory of social transformation, where consciousness, culture, political institutions and religion were wholly determined by the economic infrastructure and could thus be scientifically accounted for. In time, this tedious theory became Marxist orthodoxy. How does this 'mechanistic reductionism' differ from positivistic reductionism mentioned above? While the former approach tries to dissolve religion into its alleged infrastructural causes, the latter permits religion to stand but understands it externally in behavioural terms only.

Many Marxist thinkers have tried to regain a sense of the Marxian dialectics. They defend the relative creativity of consciousness and acknowledge that its interaction with the economic base is not devoid of surprises. Some of these thinkers, especially Ernst Bloch, have explored religion as a form of social protest, a theory Marx himself has hinted at. On the whole religion is indeed ideology. Yet Bloch recognised in apocalyptical religion the bearer of a subversive social Utopia that was prevented from historical realisation by the Church's theistic misunderstanding and came into its own through its link with infrastructural forces in the Western revolutionary tradition.[24] For Bloch, only the Western revolutionary tradition is faithful to Utopian religion, which he thought was the heart of the Scriptures. This secular tradition is 'Religion im Erbe'. While this imaginative approach overcomes mechanistic reductionism, it is still caught in systematic metaphysical negation. Bloch did not weaken his commitment to atheism.

The Marxist approach to religion offers a profound challenge to Christians and poses questions to the sociologists of religion. Even if one rejects the Marxist identification of religion with ideology and false consciousness, it cannot be denied that religion contains many ideological trends. Mainstream religion has always acted as the defender of the existing order. Some social thinkers who in no sense regard themselves as Marxists have come to distinguish in religion the ideological and the Utopian dimensions. Sociologists of religion can argue, if they so choose, that this distinction is not of primary interest to them. But Christians who study religion in terms of its fidelity to divine revelation cannot dispense themselves from listening to the critiques of religion offered by Marx and other critical thinkers. To the extent that the Christian religion legitimates unjust structures and man's domination of man it cannot represent the faith of Jesus Christ, crucified and vindicated. Critical theologians may come to feel that sociologists of religion are not helpful to theology since they study what *is* and thus attribute status and dignity to the given, while they ought to study what the given should and could be, how it can be transformed, what redemption means for it. Maybe the critical theologians will have to put brackets around Weber, Durkheim and the others until they have submitted the Christian religion to an ideological critique and tested it for authenticity. Only after this negative phase of the inquiry (if something remains of religion) will they turn to the sociologists of religion to acquire tools for a better understanding of gospel and Church in the world.

Notes

1. M. Weber *Sociology of Religion* (1922) (Boston 1964) p. 1.
2. 'Science as Vocation' *From Max Weber* ed. H. G. Gerth and C. M. Mills (New York 1958) p. 155.
3. *Sociology of Religion* p. 162.
4. E. Durkheim *Elementary Forms of the Religious Life* (1912) (New York 1965) p. 474.
5. *Ibid.* 470.
6. See. G. Baum 'Personal Testimony to Sociology' *The Ecumenist* 8 (Nov./Dec. 1969) 1-4.
7. T. Parsons 'Christianity and Modern Industrial Society' *Religion, Culture and Society* ed. L. Schneider (New York 1964) pp. 273-298.
8. R. Bellah *Beyond Belief* (New York 1970) p. 263. See also preface xv.
9. 'Civil Religion in America' *ibid.* pp. 168-192.
10. Cf. R. Tucker *Philosophy and Myth in Karl Marx* (Cambridge 1961).
11. See David Martin *The Religious and the Secular* (London 1969).
12. A. Greeley *What a Modern Catholic Believes about God* (Chicago 1971); *The New Agenda* (New York 1973).
13. P. Berger 'Some Second Thoughts on Substantive versus Functional Definitions of Religion' *Journal for the Scientific Study of Religion* 13 (1974) 125-133.
14. T. Luckmann *Invisible Religion* (New York 1967).
15. P. Berger *The Sacred Canopy* (New York 1967) pp. 136-137.
16. *Ibid.* p. 23.
17. See Roland Robertson *The Sociological Interpretation of Religion* (Oxford 1970) p. 45. Robertson has an excellent discussion of the problem of 'definitions of religion' in sociology, *ibid* pp. 34-51.
18. See *ibid.* p. 36.
19. M. Weber *Sociology of Religion* pp. 55-56.
20. P. Berger 'Secular Theology and the Rejection of the Supernatural' *Theological Studies* 38 (1977) 39.
21. P. Berger *The Sacred Canopy* pp. 100, 180.
22. R. Bellah *Beyond Belief* pp. 251.
23. Gramsci followed Croce's functionalist concept of religion. See *Selection from the Prison Notebook* ed. Q. Hoare and G. N. Smith (New York 1971) pp. 132, 344.
24. Ernst Bloch *Religion im Erbe* (Munich 1970).

PART III

Pastoral Theology and Praxis

Jacques Audinet

A Culture without Religion? The Case of France

1. The case of France appears to be clear: it is a country where religion is in process of disappearing. This is why theological debate has been forced to set out in new directions, corresponding to a quite unprecedented situation.

Of all Western countries, France does seem to be the one where the process of 'secularisation' has gone further than anywhere else. In contrast to the other Latin, or the Anglo-Saxon countries, France is a country where religion as such does not belong. Whether we talk of institutions, the identity of individuals or of social action, any religious reference is kept out of collective life.

Church and state are separated, there is no concordat, and public institutions have nothing to do with religion. The world of politics, business or education is closed to any religious intervention. If the necessities of collective life make arrangements of fact inevitable, as in the case of the schools, the latter will be referred to as private and not as religious in character. As a result France seems completely to confirm Luckmann's hypothesis that in technological societies religion becomes a private matter.

As for individuals, whether they are believers or not, they seem by common agreement to accept this situation. To the astonishment of the foreigner, the French Christian seems to be perfectly at ease in a society where the name of God is never mentioned, where religious discussion seems to be forbidden, and where nobody is ever asked his religion. Even believers are happy to think of themselves as members of a non-religious society (lay, in the French sense of this word).

In this way religion has no place in collective decisions or initiatives. It is true that over the past few years religious themes have become increasingly important in the news and the mass media of communication, but they have done so as miscellaneous facts and as entertainment items. None of this amounts to a return to religion or to a recognition of the originality of religion.

2. Faced with such a situation, theological thinking[1] has over the last few decades seen itself as grappling with 'dechristianisation', 'secularisation', 'unbelief', 'atheism' etc. . . . And the initiative here was taken by people in the field: it was the pastors between the two world wars who alerted people to 'dechristianisation' and summoned them to 'mission'. And what this amounted to was that it was no longer possible to think of society as Christian. A non-Christian 'world' existed, outside the frontiers of the Church. This world had its ideals, its values. The Church's task was not to ignore or to

condemn all this, but to proclaim the gospel to it in order to convert and transform it. These themes were opened up by Maritain and flowered in the 'pastoral theologies' which prepared the way for Vatican II. Whole sections of theological thinking in France came to turn round concepts like 'world', 'mission', 'evangelisation' and 'the Church as witness to the faith'. And a corollary of this was the rejection of what was then called 'Christendom', in the sense of a state of affairs where Church and society seemed to coincide. Anything to do with the institution was also soft-pedalled: What is important is the dynamism of mission rather than a religious apparatus, and this can be expressed in terms of an opposition between 'faith' and 'religion'. This is what seems to constitute a justification of missionary efforts. What counts is to present the message in all its purity to an atheist world. 'Religion', on the other hand, is a human phenomenon which secretes many ambiguous forms of expression that vary according to different societies and cultures. The authentic gospel is seen as something that *breaks with* social forms of religion and it is open to being 'demythologised' itself. This is how a way opens up for a theology based on the Word breaking with 'culture'. The events which found it, whether in history—the death and resurrection of Jesus—or in the lives of individuals—conversion—as well as the language that expresses it somehow escape from the religious mechanisms of human cultures. They are 'transcendent' of themselves.

There is another current too: that of theologies of history and political theology. Faced with the incontestable fact of a society without religion, they seek to discern mediations of Christian revelation—this time, however, not in the absolute of a word breaking with culture, but in the manifestations and travail of history. The adventures of man is where salvation occurs. On this basis, human situations, earthly realities, political stuggles become the privileged places of disclosure of Christian salvation, although it is not always very clear how this process (which is, nevertheless, the basis of Christian 'commitment') actually works.

So, faced with a culture without religion, the two ways in which Christians attempt to define their attitudes in France are in terms of *breaking* or *conniving* with such a culture. In practice, of course, these two overlap. How, then, do they often lead into dead-ends?

3. The reason is that in a country like France the relationship between culture and religion is much more complicated than might at first sight appear. When brought to the test of reality, the policies of both break and connivance lead to unexpected results. Thus a word, which would like to present itself as a word of faith breaking with culture, is often heard as a piece of archaic or ethical language which fails to convey its essential mystical import and dimension. In a similar way a testimony that sets out to be shared and available to everybody is often received as the expresssion of the life-style of a restricted group, let alone of some élite inspired by an ideology.

Culture is not a neutral receptacle in relation to religion. It proffers a series of representations, values, and attitudes which interact with forms of actual religious behaviour. Religion, on the other hand, does not exist in a pure state, as a set of invariable pronouncements or norms. Religious forms are themselves the product of cultural elaborations of given times and epochs, beginning with those of the people to whom revelation was first given. To overlook this is to condemn oneself to wanting to speak a word independently of the symbols, representations and values which it brings into play. It amounts to denying the preconditions of speech in the very act of speaking, that is to say, to condemn oneself to verbiage or to aphasia. It is to make a show of Christian life outside whatever at any given period makes up the elements of any human existence, that is to say, to end up on the fringe of things.

We therefore begin to see that it is just too simple to conceive of the relationship between culture and religion as if we had, on the one hand, culture without religion, and, on the other, religion purged of any cultural element. Practical experience revealed the complexity of things and so soon made such formal concepts inherited from the

Enlightenment relative. It is more a question of seeing how, in each case, any particular religious form emerges, is transformed and impinges upon a given situation.

In this regard, France constitutes an excellent laboratory, for it is a country in which institutionalised Catholicism was dominant for over a millenium, but it is also a country where whole areas of culture have emerged and developed outside, if not against, the religious view of life. But institutionalised religion no longer enfolds society; it is only one element among others in the fan of social forces whilst new religious energies appear outside it or at its edges. What is more, the cultural universes constituted by the worlds of science, politics and social action are in themselves a-religious. And they will remain so since history does not go backwards. At the same time, they are experiencing the emergence of certain questions about social bonding, the identity of individuals or the purpose of life which may not be religious in the classical sense of the word but which do correspond to traditionally religious concerns. The various situations in France do, then, consist of a mingling of elements which need to be sorted out. Recent research is beginning to shed light on the variety and complexity of the French cultural and religious landscape. These pieces of research are coming out of the various sciences of society: history, sociology, ethnology. They are extremely relevant to the question which concerns us here, because they compel us to think of religion in a different way, but also enable us to think of culture in a correspondingly different way.[2]

4. We can indicate three domains in which recent research work brings the *complexity and paradoxes* of the situation in France to light.

The first concerns the *identity of individuals*. Collective life in our country may well be a-religious and yet most individuals have recourse, at least on occasions in their lives, to religious gestures. Religious baptisms and funerals are still mass phenomena for large sections of the population. Things are changing, and especially in the large urban agglomerations where religious gestures are manifestly on the decline. There are, however, new phenomena: the emergence of strong Muslim communities, a renewal of Judaism and the development of sects, all of which goes to show that the alternative is not simply a switch from Catholicism or Protestantism on a large scale to non-religion. France has long been characterised by religious unity but now seems well on the way to becoming a country of religious pluralism. And this means that we can no longer define individuals as a function of religious institutions. As F. Boulard wrote in 1968: 'In the years to come religious practice as defined by the Church could well be an indicator worth watching. It is one of the main ways in which, through the so-called phenomenon of the "third man", we can see a silent movement of detachment from religious life as organised into a Church and from the obligations which this imposes.'[3] Detachment from the religious institution—in France, the Catholic Church—is not identical with the disappearance of religion. Society no longer believes in this institutionalisation of religion so much. It does not, however, necessarily follow that individuals abandon all religious concern.

A second example concerns the influence of religion in realms from which it is in principle banned in French society. I have in mind in particular the *political realm*. Recent studies disclose the way religion and politics are mixed up with each other in contemporary France. What is in question here is not 'games of influence' between people in authority; it is a deeper matter of the way in which a given form of religious adherence seems to form a certain type of political animal. This is why there is a sort of Catholic 'sub-culture' in France just as there is a certain sort of communist 'sub-culture'. For a member of any such sub-culture the diverse elements which go to make it up belong together—in the case of Catholics, for instance, faith, a certain sense of the family and a tendency to vote conservative. The upshot of this—and this again is paradoxical—is that the most secular area of French life, that is to say, political life, begins to appear to be in it depths not untouched by religion. This may be an accident of history, but political scientists know that it is worth their particular attention because it too is in flux. The relationship between politics and religion may be denied verbally but it continues to operate culturally. It touches upon society's deepest will to live.[4]

A third area of research seems to be particularly fertile at present. It is at the intersection of the historical and social sciences and is concerned *to bring mentalities to light* and to see how they evolve in countries like France. What is meant by mentality here is everything that touches upon beliefs and general collective attitudes. Studies of death, fear, festival, village life, work, abound.[5] They are in the form of learned works but they are often also monographs which are best-sellers. Their success shows that the rapid economic development of the last decades brings with it a need to refind collective identity. And what do we discover here? We discover that the roots of collective identity in a country like France are soaked in religion. The rhythms of time, social links, the image of life and death, as well as that of morality, love and power, in other words, all the great identifying symbols of this secularised country are stamped by centuries of religion. The notion of 'popular religion' which has been reinstated over these past few years is in the same line: the recovery of that collective identity which was assured in the past by the integrating religious manifestations of culture such as pilgrimage, procession and devotions. Recent work shows the complexity of the phenomenon, as well as its ambiguity and its mobility. The archaic is still with us, and it is not enough to reproduce it for it to be quickening.

5. Something quite different is in question. We begin to see that in a country like France the relationship between culture and religion is very complex. And the first result of the work we have just alluded to is to put both the practical man and the theologian on their guard against any ideological over-simplification. That, however, is not all: becoming aware of the way in which culture and religion inter-relate opens up new possibilities at once for action and for thought. What we need in the first place is analysis. As soon as we start from the relationship between culture and religion as it actually exists in practice, we come to see that in any given country complexes that are both cultural and religious have developed over the centuries, and we can call these the 'socio-historic faces of Christianity'. We need to take stock of them. This is where thought as well as action begins. These complexes are in movement, what Maurice Bellet calls 'the displacement of religion'.[6] What we need to understand is the transformation involved. It is not, therefore, so much a question of a 'return of the sacred', or of a global and definitive secularisation, as of new faces of social and religious life. Such faces include the Christian ones that emerge as so many possibilities, and they may be given in a tradition or they may need to be recreated. These Christian faces, such as speech, the institution, rites, constitute so many cultural products susceptible of analysis, which can include the specific aspects of the Christian tradition which they represent. The desire to bring them to life today supposes a reworking of concepts and forms of action calculated to express in terms of contemporary systems of representation, social links and symbolism what the tradition carries. This is the task of what some people call 'practical theology',[7] that is to say, a theology which sees itself as the theory of that original social behaviour which is constituted by the behaviour of believers. It seeks to exploit the contribution of the critical sciences and, in full acknowledgement of the irreversible secularisation, to make the word of belief heard.

This is the sort of task we need to address ourselves to in a country like France where religion, according to some authors, is full of dynamism whilst, according to others, it is in shreds. It is a task calling for intelligence, imagination and initiative. It is on the way that such a task is carried through that the future and destiny of the religious adventure turns.

Translated by Iain McGonagle

Notes

1. See Claude Geffré *Un nouvel âge de la théologie* (Paris 1972).
2. See Michel Meslin *Pour une Science des religions* (Paris 1973).
3. F. Boulard *Pratique religieuse et régions culturelles* (Paris 1968) p. 183.
4. See Guy Michelat, Michel Simon *Classes, religion et comportement politique* (Paris 1977).
5. See, for example, Jean Delumeau *La Peur en occident* (Paris 1978).
6. Maurice Bellet *Le Déplacement de la Religion* (Paris 1972).
7. Rene Marle *Le projet de théologie pratique* (Paris 1979).

Segundo Galilea

The Theology of Liberation and the Place of 'Folk Religion'

FOR VERY many years the fact of 'folk religion' was accepted as a habitual part of Christianity on the continent of Latin America and not regarded as a worthy object of discussion. The last three decades, however, have seen it elevated to an object of concern and debate, on the part of both pastoral theology and social science.

This development has—in general terms—coincided with the emergence of the theme of liberation in social struggles for justice, and therefore in the pastoral theology and practice of the Church. The liberation of the poor and the oppressed became the prime concern of Christians.[1] This has led the greater part of the Church in an 'exodus' towards the world of the poor. On a deep level, there has been a coming together of Church leaders and theologians with the people, with its miseries and exploitation, with its just struggle and aspirations, and therefore, inevitably, with its religious instinct.

This is what lies behind the coexistence and convergence of the themes of liberation and folk religion in Christian thinking. Both are typical of the task facing Christians on this continent and special to it. The matter could be put like this: the subjects of our liberation endeavours—the poor and the oppressed—live their own form of folk religion, which is most usually expressed in Catholic categories; it is a popular Catholicism.

1. THE COMPLEXITY OF FOLK RELIGION

The characteristics of Latin American folk religion (Catholicism) are well-known to pastoral workers and theologians.[2] They seem to agree on its close identification with the simple and the poor, forming one of the basic substrata of their culture ('cultural' Catholicism). It is conditioned by the poverty, insecurity and oppression of the people; it is a 'religion of poverty', both in its origins, which lie in the Iberian Catholicism of the Counter-reformation, influenced by the folk religions of the native Indians and Afro-American negroes, and in its ecclesial situation: it is a Catholicism more or less cut off from the liturgy and official pastoral directives, with generally decadent characteristics—which does not prevent it from being persistent and lively, nor from preserving genuinely Christian values (its attitude to life and death, its sense of solidarity and the divine, etc.).

Its expressions and manifestations are also well known; these often coincide with those of traditional religious cultures: devotionalism, attachment to sacred places, things and rituals; the value placed on religious symbols (of a Catholic cast); trust in God and his saints, whose intercession is sometimes expected direct; human fellowship and solidarity in human relations, etc. . . .

All this leads to three overall conclusions: (*a*) Latin American folk religion is today deeply-rooted and flourishing, despite the deep social and cultural changes of the past few decades; (*b*) this folk religion is very complex, since an analysis and understanding of it require other factors besides purely religious and pastoral-catechetical ones to be taken into account: those proper to the popular culture in which it is enveloped, those linked to underdevelopment and marginalisation, those stemming from popular tradition, symbology and the collective unconscious, etc.; (*c*) Latin American folk religion is deeply ambiguous; evaluating it from a Christian standpoint is a complex process because of its mixture of motivations and attitudes, which vary in value from the Christian to the syncretist, from 'charity religion' to 'self-interest religion'.

Latin American theologians and pastoral workers seem to have reached a consensus on these conclusions and on the fact that popular Catholicism belongs to the substratum of the cultures and dynamics leading to the liberation of the people. These same conclusions lie at the base of discussion of folk religion in its meeting with the liberation needs of this same oppressed people.

2. LIBERATION QUESTIONS FOR FOLK RELIGION

In this frame of reference, the theology of liberation, which seeks to inspire a sense of their dignity and rights in the poor people of Latin America, to imbue them with a critical consciousness of their situation of poverty and oppression, to give them a Christian motivation for working together for their advancement and liberation instead of resigning themselves for false reasons and conforming to the secular norm, cannot but pose some sharp questions in relation to folk religion. The thrust of this questioning will not be whether folk religion is capable of surviving or of keeping the people believing in a secularised world, as it would be in highly industrialised countries, but whether it is capable of being a positive factor in the liberation of the poor.

The questions concern the theology of liberation and Christian practice of liberation. Whether reasonably or not, whether from a broad or narrow base (this debate is part of the discussion we are analysing), folk religion has from the last three decades been examined on points ranging from its basic Christian identity to its role in relation to liberation. Is it a valid starting-point for liberation? Or does it rather lead to conformity and alienation? Can a critical and changing consciousness be developed from folk religion, or must it always be a stage of development that has to be surpassed? Do pastoral care of folk religion and liberating evangelisation converge or diverge in their aims and practice? And supposing that folk religion is a factor that cannot be overlooked in the practice of liberation, is this for purely tactical reasons or because it really is a potentially liberating factor?

Such a line of questioning leads to the most radical of all: To what extent can Latin American folk religion in its present manifestation be called genuinely Christian? Should we not divide this religion from 'liberating and genuine' Christianity with which the theology of liberation is identified? In this case, the religion of the people would only 'formally' be Christian; it would be the religious expression of a people expressing itself in Christian rites and symbols because these are the only ones it knows, the only ones its society and culture provide it with.

The different replies that have been given to these questions, from the standpoint of Christian liberation, form the subject-matter of this article.

3. THE CRITICAL EVALUATION

The first evaluations of folk religion date from the 1950's. At first, religious sociologists, theologians and (most) pastoral workers were united in a negative view. At this time, the theme of liberation as such had not come into its own; criticism was influenced by other considerations, such as the need to foment militant and committed movements and communities in the Church of Latin America, thereby accentuating a Christianity of élites and a Church capable of being an evangelical sign and witness. From this standpoint popular religion was seen as a grey, murky area of Christianity. This line of thought is still operative in certain quarters.[3]

At this time, those who accepted, to a greater or lesser extent, the postulates of North American 'secularisation theology', agreed with this highly critical evaluation. This current implied (or was understood in Latin America to imply) a secularised Christianity, standing aside from traditional religious forms of expression. The difference between Christianity and 'popular religion' was strongly stressed, with the latter seen as being inevitably in a process of continual decline, which was not seen as much of a loss for Christianity in Latin America, where popular religious expression was seen in terms of 'natural religion' or 'cultural religion' expressed in Catholic forms. It was seen as a superficial Christianity, far removed from life and historical tasks.[4]

More recently, when the whole question of liberation and its accompanying theology were introduced, this critical evaluation of folk religion was taken up by those who favoured Marxist analysis. Popular religious expression was contrasted with the conditions necessary for liberation, and it was criticised on the lines of Marxist condemnation of all religion. This was the most secularised current in the 'theology' of liberation. It accentuated the differences between 'liberating Christianity' (which it exempted from general strictures on religion) and 'popular religion', whose historical role was seen as alienating the poor from the possibility of a critical and mobilising consciousness.

The cause of this alienation, however, was not seen in the hold religion had over the people, but in the economic and ideological manipulation introduced into Latin American religious consciousness by the situation of domination and dependence. In a two-sided process, popular religion at once made the oppressed find their situation of exploitation acceptable through its symbolic structure (of evasion and resignation), which was fomented by the dominant culture and the ruling classes, and at the same time injected the ideology of these ruling classes into the consciousness of the people, thereby reinforcing their dependence on the secular level. The question of whether this popular religion was or was not Christianity followed from this analysis: at best it would be the projection of an ideologised Christianity, incompatible with the consciousness and practice of liberation.

Given the influence of Marxist categories (which made the overthrow of the capitalist system the ultimate liberation) in this line of thought, the question of the pastoral value of popular religion was virtually meaningless. For strategic reasons, or out of human respect, it would not be frontally criticised or alienated, but would be set aside and dissolved (at least in theory) in a process of economic and political liberation.[5]

At the present stage reached in the discussion of the problem of liberation in relation to folk religion, this position is quite definitely a minority one. The tendency of liberation theologians and pastoral theorists is now to take a much more positive view of popular religion as a manifestation of Christianity and as a potential force for liberation. But within this positive current there are also differences of emphasis and evaluation.

4. FOLK RELIGION AS KEY TO CULTURAL LIBERATION

Earlier positions laid stress on socio-economic liberation and their ideological consequences in their judgements of popular religion. This generated a critical reaction, which questioned the postulates behind the earlier judgements and came to see religious feeling as a positive force for the liberation of the poor. This reaction was largely the work of the 'cultural' current of the theology of liberation, most prominent in the Argentine school, but with adherents elsewhere, principally Chile and Brazil.[6]

This school maintains that the deepest constituent of the Latin American people is its culture—popular culture or cultures. Defence of the values of this culture, threatened by ideological domination and socio-economic oppression, is a defence of the soul and the roots of the people, the sources of its freedom. Liberation, in the final analysis, must be a cultural liberation, a blanket notion embracing liberation from economic and social dominations as well as from ideologies that alienate and crush popular culture.

These ideologies are seen as originating in the North Atlantic sphere, belonging to the world of 'enlightened' and secularising modernity. They belong to 'élitist' cultures in Latin America, as opposed to the popular cultures. 'Élitist' culture is domineering and invades popular culture in the shape of liberalism, capitalism, consumerism—and also Marxism. The peoples of Latin America, rooted in their own cultural identity, should bring about their liberation without selling their souls to élitist, secularising and Northern ideologies.

Now the fact is that popular religion (Catholicism) is an essential part of popular cultures; it therefore forms part of the identity of the people. Even more, in many parts it is the most creative and original part of the people's heritage, and, throughout a continent culturally taken over and dominated by 'élites' from inside and outside, forms the great cultural and spiritual reservoir of the oppressed. So if liberation is to be liberation of their culture, folk religion, whatever its ambiguities, plays an important and positive role in this process.

Critical evaluations of religious expression are in their turn criticised as being 'élitist' and prejudiced. The marked differentiation between folk religion and Christianity is unjust: it leaves out of account the fact that there is no 'ideal model' of Christianity, which has always been and is always expressed through the medium of a particular culture. The cultural expression of Christianity in Latin America is its popular religion. It is true that this religion has its failings and ambiguities, but not markedly more so than other cultural forms of Catholicism regarded as more 'developed' by the dominant cultures.

The presumed incompatibility between liberation and religious expression is also criticised as prejudiced by an ideological view of liberation, opposed to the liberation that stems from the people and its culture. Liberation cannot be brought about without uniting the struggle for socio-economic justice with a consciousness of one's own culture; which makes it impossible to leave folk religion out of account, since it is the Christian (and therefore potentially liberating) constituent of popular culture.

5. FOLK RELIGION AS POTENTIAL FOR SOCIO-ECONOMIC LIBERATION

Not all the currents in liberation thinking that value folk religion would identify with this viewpoint. There is an equally important school which stresses the political factor in the practice of liberation, i.e., popular organisation and the formation of a popular power base—antecedent to any ideological commitment. Here Christian and political education are the vital tasks. Though popular culture and its liberation are not to be neglected, they have to be set in the context of socio-political liberation. Folk religion is here seen as retaining its potential value, but less in relation to culture and more in relation to its capacity for strengthening the political consciousness and mobilisation of the people. (Needless to say, though I am making a schematic distinction here between two schools, in practice and in their writings they shade into each other and often overlap.)

For this 'second' school, folk religion is less decidedly positive than for the first. Its liberating potential needs to be proven, so pastoral approaches to it, and the process of 'conscientisation' are all-important. And while there is more criticism of the failures and ambiguities of popular religion, and its risks of alienation, its identification with Christianity is not called into question. Whether from considerations of pastoral strategy or from a valuative conviction, this school (like the first) insists on the indissolubility of the dual condition of the people of Latin America: an exploited people and a Christian people. This makes it possible for liberation to be Christian and for the religion of the people to be liberating. For this last to come about, the people have to be 'politicised', to purify their popular religion of alienating tendencies and free it from infection by the 'ideologised Christianity' of the ruling classes.

This school is important in Mexico, El Salvador, Peru and parts of Brazil and Chile.[7]

6. FOLK RELIGION IN LIBERATING EVANGELISATION

There is one point—and a most important one—on which all theologians of liberation with any pastoral sense agree: that from whichever point of view one approaches the question, folk religion has to be the object of a process of liberating evangelisation if it is to develop a consciousness of change and a spirituality of liberation in the people.[8]

In effect, from the pastoral standpoint, there is now a majority consensus in Latin America, which makes the debate on popular religion and liberation less acute. Liberation theologians are agreed in seeing the religion of the people as basically Christian—therefore containing a liberating dynamism—though at present ambiguous and conditioned by oppression—and therefore capable of deviating and playing an alienating role.

Popular religion will be either liberating or alienating depending on the quality of its aims and content—and this is a pastoral challenge. If evangelisation does not strengthen a liberating spirituality, the liberation of the oppressed will take place 'in spite of' or even 'against' the religion of the people. If evangelisation is liberating (which in general terms means productive of a critical spirit of solidarity, a feeling for one's own dignity and a sense of Christianity as commitment and justice), liberation will be brought about 'on the basis of' popular Catholicism (though this will not be its only basis).

In any case, the discussion, on the theological and the pastoral level, of the question of the relationship between liberation and folk religion has already borne one important fruit: evangelisation in Latin America is now conscious of the need to reinterpret the expression and symbols of the religion of the people in a spirit of liberation (Puebla, 469).

Translated by Paul Burns

Notes

1. This imperative—commitment to the poor—has been the official position of the Church in Latin America from Medellín to Puebla.

2. Among the abundant works on the subject are: *Religiosidad popular e Iglesia* (Bogatá 1977); S. Galilea *Religiosidad popular y pastoral* (Madrid 1979); Conference of Puebla *The Evangelisation of Popular Religion*.

3. J. L. Segundo *La Pastoral latinoamericana. Sus motivos ocultos* (Montevideo 1972) and *Esa comunidad llamada Iglesia* (Buenos Aires 1977).

4. This trend is summarised in E. Pin *Introducción a la sociologia del catolicismo latinoamericano* (Bogotá 1962).

5. What is expressed schematically here is not always directly apparent from the relevant books, e.g., H. Assman *A Practical Theology of Liberation* (London and New York 1976), and the early writings of the Chilean 'Christians for Socialism' group.

6. Boasso *Qué es la pastoral popular* (Buenos Aires 1975); J. Scanone 'Teología, cultura popular y discernimiento' in *La nueva frontera de la teología en America Latina* (Salamanca 1977); *idem. Teologia de la liberación y praxis popular* (Salamanca 1976); E. Hoornaert *Historia do catolicismo popular brasileiro* (Petropolis 1978); various *Religiosidad y cultura* (Santiago de Chile 1977).

7. There are no full-length works on this theme, but articles in reviews published in Brazil, Mexico and Peru, especially *Christus* (Mexico), May 1979, are devoted to folk religion.

8. See the Conference of Medellín *Pastoral Popular* nn. 8, 11-15; Conference of Puebla nn. 479, 482, 483, 485, 1134, 1137, 1146, 1164 and especially 452, 457-459. These official texts sum up the thought now common to all theologians and pastoral workers in Latin America.

Martin Marty

North America: The Empirical Understanding of Religion and Theology

BOTH IN folk usage and scholarly discourse, North Americans distinguish clearly between 'religion' and 'theology'. The definitions of theology tend to be more narrow and precise, whereas with good reason religion tends to be protean and diffuse and therefore deserving of more attention.

1. CIVIL DEFINITIONS OF RELIGION

While Canada thinks of itself as a bicultural and bireligious society, the United States prides itself in its wild pluralism. Yet its citizens do tend to cherish religious self-definitions of the sort provided by Mr Justice Douglas of the United States Supreme Court:[1] 'We are a religious people whose institutions presuppose a Supreme Being.' The latter half of that dictum is arguable, but both those who favour and those who oppose religion agree that by conventional measures Americans 'are a religious people'. How do they define religion?

The same Supreme Court, while it lacks official authority to do so, has contributed on the highest level of symbolism to periodic definitions of religion. Thus Chief Justice Hughes, dissenting in *United States* v. *MacIntosh*,[2] wrote that 'the essence of religion is belief in a relation to God involving duties superior to those arising from any human relation'. In 1948 the Congress in a statute carried the definition into the legislative branch: 'Religious training and belief . . . mean an individual's belief in relation to a Supreme Being involving duties superior to those arising from any human relation. . . .'

These governmental definitions, which lack binding power, were uncontroversial when first written. They match some that come from the theological community. Thus Julian N. Hartt has written that 'we ought to say that a man is not really religious unless he feels that some power is bearing down on him, unless, that is, he believes he must do something about divine powers who have done something about him'. To this James M. Gustafson has added an elaboration: 'I reserve the word "religious" for that dimension of experience (in which not all persons consciously share) that senses a relationship to an ultimate power that sustains and stands over against humans in the world.'[3]

These tend to be middle-range definitions. Since 1948 the Supreme Court has greatly broadened its understanding of what religion is, particularly in a case involving selective conscientious objection to the military draft. In *United States* v. *Seeger*,[4] the judges showed that they had been reading theologian Paul Tillich, who used a broader definition. Religion had only to include 'a sincere and meaningful belief which occupies in the life of its possessor a place parallel to that filled by . . . God . . .'. The Seeger Court used a dictionary definition of a Supreme Being to rule that he was *not* integral to religions such as Buddhism, or the faith of appellant Seeger: 'a power or being, or a faith, "to which all else is subordinate or upon which all else is ultimately dependent".'

2. THE MOST BROAD AND MOST NARROW VIEWS

While it would be hard to come up with empirical data to reinforce the notion, the listener to common speech and the reader of endless documentation are likely to conclude that religion *minus* 'divine powers' or 'ultimate power' or 'Supreme Being' is constitutionally necessary but not very helpful or frequent in mundane speech. The public is tolerant but not necessarily comprehending when the academic person resorts to the very widely accepted anthropological definition of religion by Clifford Geertz: 'A religion is: (1) a system of symbols which acts to (2) establish powerful, pervasive, and long-lasting moods and motivations in men by (3) formulating conceptions of a general order of existence and (4) clothing these conceptions with such an aura of factuality that (5) the moods and motivations seem uniquely realistic.'[5] Yet in practice they do think of as religion various non-theisms like Ethical Culture, humanistic Unitarianism, Zen Buddhism, 'anything which has a "church"', and many occult phenomena.

If the courts have used moderate definitions and the academy broad ones, there are also large numbers of people who survey the pluralism and with sectarian pride are very restrictive: religion is the religion of the churches, preferably of their own church. Historian Sidney E. Mead, defending 'the religion of the republic' against the people he calls 'temple-ists', derides them by importing the example of Parson Thwackum from the English novelist Henry Fielding:[6]

> When I mention religion I mean the Christian religion; and not only the Christian religion, and not only the Protestant religion, but the Church of England. And when I mention honour, I mean that mode of Divine grace which is not only consistent with, but dependent upon, this religion; and is consistent with and dependent upon no other.

To all but the Thwackumites, the definition of religion need not include any specific content, though there is some wavering between those who include 'powers' or 'God' and those who do not. Having invoked the judicial and legislative branches of government, it is in order now to refer to the executive, since it is American presidents who have often played priestly roles in enacting and defining American religion. Not many twentieth-century presidents were more admired that Dwight D. Eisenhower. To our knowledge, few citizens protested when he spelled out the functions of contentless religion in pluralist America. Thus: 'Our government makes no sense unless it is founded in a deeply felt religious faith—and I don't care what it is.' Having religion was more important than having a substance of faith.

Students of the Canadian experience find religion more related to institutions like churches and synagogues than to the national experience. Canada lacked a revolution as a congealing experience; its confederation in 1867 was a generally quiet affair that generated few symbols. Catholic Quebec provides such a different framework for civil life from the rest of Canada that the two cannot easily meet. And much of the United States's generalised religiosity, which has no civil counterpart in Canada, developed as a result of the Enlightenment, an event that was less marked or intense in Canada.

3. THE LOCATION OF THEOLOGY

In both nations, theology is ordinarily seen in relation to the life of the churches and not the civil society, though there have been tendencies of late in the United States to speak of a 'public theology'. If theology is the interpretation of the language of a believing community, it can come from either direction: ecclesiastical figures reflecting on the activity of God beyond the churchly community are public theologians, while public philosophers who deal with the transcendental language of the republic in their reflection could also be conceived of as public theologians.

In the empirical situation of America, past and present, theology connotes a professional discipline which occurs chiefly in the academy. While it is true that some of the foremost theologians in American history such as Jonathan Edwards and Horace Bushnell spent virtually all or a substantial portion of their careers in parishes, and while some devoted years to the parish (Walter Rauschenbusch, Reinhold Niebuhr), today theology is what professors write. In a recent study of 558 theologians, 50·98 per cent were employed in seminaries and theological schools, 16·24 per cent in college or university contexts, and only 2·51 per cent were in pastoral, executive, or editorial posts outside the academy.[7]

North American religion is often described as activistic and pragmatic. In *A Nation of Behavers* (Chicago: University of Chicago 1977) I have shown how far one can go in interpreting American religion by reference to behaviour rather than to belief and to the cognitive dimensions on which theologians rely. This predisposition has produced a hard to document but still manifest presence of a condescending attitude toward theology. Such a circumscription of it has many rationales, and we should look at a few of them.

4. NEGATIVE VIEWS OF THEOLOGY

First, theology is intellectual, and the intellect is only one dimension of human life. The theologian looks to critics like one who concentrates on only that dimension at the expense of experience and activity, both of which receive a higher premium in America. Second, it was long believed that while action unites, doctrine divides. With over 220 religious groups in the *Yearbook of American and Canadian Churches*, the public has always been concerned to impose tolerant or ecumenical attitudes on as many of the churches as possible. While the most sectarian of the churches, like Jehovah's Witnesses and the Latter-Day Saints are the fastest growing and are often admired for the devotion they inspire among their adherents, they are regarded as luxuries in an otherwise more tolerant republic. But given the *odium theologicum* of the past, citizens do not welcome the prospect that precisionists of dogmatists' temper would add to tension in national life.

While Canadians have been more tolerant of religious differences in education than have people of the United States, even to the point that they subsidised religious schools, they have generally lacked the Enlightenment spirit which in the era of its founding led the United States's leaders to express distrust of theology. To Thomas Paine and Thomas Jefferson, no less than to many British deists or French or German ideologues of the eighteenth century, organised religion meant priestcraft and superstition. Theologians dealt with *hocus-pocus*, intellectual contrivances to justify their way of life.

Add to these reasons the passion for simplicity that has characterised not only Protestant but other religious life in America. The bewilderments of pluralism have led to what Peter Gay calls a 'hunger for wholeness'. This hunger leads to frequent appeals for 'just the simple gospel', 'childlike faith', or direct recourse to literal biblical or papal authority. The theologians raise complicated questions. The primitive impulse is linked to a certain mistrust of professionalism in religion. While the typical North American expects the medical doctor to use the most technical language possible, the expert in religion is seen as an obfuscator or traducer if he or she deals in arcane and difficult language.

During the past decade any number of Marxist and other interpreters of the rise of professionalism have argued that near the end of the nineteenth century—when theology moved from church to university—self-preserving élites in Protestantism devised a meritocracy, complete with jargon to keep non-experts at a distance. In Catholicism the trend became visible somewhat later.[8]

From out of that period has come a classic statement of the distinction academics made between religion and theology. Andrew Dickson White, president of Cornel University, insisted that there be no sectarian influence or theology department at his university. In the introduction to his celebrated *A History of the Warfare of Science with Theology in Christendom*,[9] White showed how the two were related to science. 'My conviction is that science, though it has evidently conquered dogmatic theology based on biblical texts and ancient modes of thought, will go hand in hand with religion; and that, although theological control will continue to diminish, religion, as seen in the recognition of "a power in the universe, not ourselves, which makes for righteousness", and in the love of God and of our neighbour, will steadily grow stronger and stronger, not only in the American institutions of learning but in the world at large.'

5. THEOLOGY AND ITS COMMUNITIES

A century later—White wrote his early drafts in the 1870's—some of the old belligerence has disappeared. Today the religion of common people is mistrustful of many scientific claims, while it is the theologians who relate positively to science. Yet if the pejorative character has waned, thanks in part to the celebrity status of post-Vatican II theologians who showed themselves to be more 'open' than religionists, distinctions themselves remain necessary.

While one never hears the term 'theology' used in the case of native American religion—though a thinker like Vine Deloria, Jr., author of *God Is Red*, definitely writes non-Christian theology—the black community lives with both categories. Black religion is an amalgam of the inheritance brought from Africa but almost lost in slavery, slave adaptations of owners' religion, and autochthonous orthodox Christian appropriations by black church leaders. In the 1960's, black leaders like James Cone and Deotis Roberts, Sr., began to speak of 'black theology'. Thus James H. Cone wrote *Liberation: A Black Theology of Liberation*.[10] Such thinkers made a distinction between 'folk' expression and the formal language of interpretation that is called theology.

Judaism historically has not felt at home with the term theology, seeing it connote a Greek-Christian ethos. The laws, symbols, and history by which Jews lived made up its religion. But in America the narrative and practice of faith demanded interpretation. So there is a Jewish Theological Seminary, and Jews play their part in American pluralism by participating in theological enterprises.[11]

One could pursue the religion/theology distinction through other communities, such as that of the feminists. Feminist religion tends to be an expression of impulses that draw their exemplars from the feminine principle in godhead and human experience. Feminist theology is an intellectual extrapolation on that experience. It is more interesting to see a change in the understanding of their roles on the part of theologians.

6. NEW THEOLOGICAL ROLES AND COMMUNITIES

Twenty years ago and more, especially in North American Catholicism, to say 'theologian' was to suggest a dogmatic custodian of magisterial truth. When the theologian was in the direct service of ecclesiastical institutions, whether as monk, bishop, or seminary professor, such a custodial role was natural. Thanks to the professional revolution, which moved half the practising theologians to the secular academy—Catholics joined this revolution after the Second Vatican Council—they began to become responsible to the university and to each other. Thus it was natural for them to be responsive to norms once thought to be alien to theology. And the impetus to innovate grew. Only three years after the Council, when Pope Paul VI issued *Humanae Vitae*, there was an almost instant declaration by hundreds of professional Catholic theologians, including those employed in seminaries, calling into question papal and episcopal reasoning. This would have been unheard of before the Council, though Protestants had grown used to such dynamics in their churches before the turn of the century, when professional theologians more than parish pastors promoted liberal and modernist thought. There is more psychic and intellectual disengagement and mobility in the academy. Whereas Andrew Dickson White had pictured theology as the retardant to religious progress, now religiosity was the force of inertia holding theology back. The 'death of God' expression in the mid-sixties was a sign of this adaptability and innovative spirit. It was almost unthinkable in folk religion. A Chicago butchers' union bannered on its marquee a phrase passers-by could easily grasp: 'God is Dead, Theologians Say. Not our God.'

Along with this shift in roles there has been a broadening of the linguistic repertory of theologians. The believing community to which each related used to be bounded by one's own communion or sectarian history. The ecumenical and interfaith movements have made it possible and necessary to account for larger experiences. The pronouns have changed, thanks to the feminist movement. The hopes and memories of Christian theology sound different because of some decades of encounter with 'post-Holocaust' Jewish thought. To this I would add the language of the American public religion, which has been in eclipse during the 1970's.

7. INDIVIDUALISED RELIGION AND THEOLOGY

Both religion and theology have grown more complex during recent years as America joined other post-industrial societies in seeing religion turn more individualistic and become more of a 'private affair'. While religious institutions remain comparatively healthy in America, during the past decade there has been more growth of clienteles and convergences than of congregations and denominations. Celebrities evoke *ad hoc* followings over television and radio or through best-selling paperback books or personal appearances. Each of them develops his or her own language for conversion, healing, or the offering of goods. As such, they do not tend to spawn fresh theology, since the communities are insufficiently stable for the theologians.

Meanwhile, the theologians have moved increasingly into the secular academy, where they cannot use a church or even the church as an automatic reference group. In the seminaries, the people they addressed at least presumably shared a common confession. In the pluralistic academy they have to construct a world of meanings before they can exeget it. During the years of that shift we have not had as vital a theological community as the one that emerged during the years of Protestant neo-orthodoxy, when the churches were more intact and their legitimacy was taken for granted. And the Second Vatican Council also gave rise to a more vital Catholic theology than we see now. Today the theologians are in search of the language they will have to interpret. The science of hermeneutics grows. The issue of who or what to construe and expound continues to trouble the interpreters. Yet awareness of this plight may give stimulus to new creativity; such upheavals in the past have led not always to malaise but sometimes to innovation.

Notes

1. *Zorach* v. *Clauson* 343 U.S. 306, 72 S.Ct. 679, 96 L.Ed. 954.
2. 283 U.S. 605, 633, 1931.
3. James M. Gustafson *The Contributions of Theology to Medical Ethics* (Milwaukee 1975) p. 97.
4. 380 U.S. 163, 1965.
5. In *The Religious Situation 1968* ed. Donald R. Cutler (Boston 1968) p. 643.
6. Sidney E. Mead *The Nation with the Soul of a Church* (New York 1975) p. 8.
7. Thor Hall *Systematic Theology Today: The State of the Art in North America* Part I (Washington 1978) p. 38.
8. On the culture of professionalism in general, see Burton Bledstein *The Culture of Professionalism: The Middle Class and the Development of Higher Education in America* (New York 1976).
9. 1896; modern edition (New York 1975) p. 27.
10. (New York 1979). James J. Gardiner and J. Deotis Roberts, Sr. pursued the *Quest for a Black Theology* (Philadelphia 1970).
11. See for example, Arthur Cohen *The Natural and the Supernatural Jew: An Historical and Theological Introduction* (New York 1962) for an apologia for Jewish theology.

Matthew Lamb

The Christian Religion as Mystical and Political in Germany

IT IS presumptuous for a foreigner, even one who did his graduate studies there, to report briefly on the significance of contemporary developments in the practice and theory of religion in Germany. Nevertheless, editorial requests often have the habit of transforming presumption into prescriptions. From the perspective of contemporary sociologies of religion—especially those dominated by an empirical functionalism—what strikes the outsider is how deceptive appearances are. Contemporary Germany should appear to be a country of contradictions. The state socialism in East Germany and the late capitalism in West Germany are hailed as exemplary realisations of the two supposedly antithetical socio-economic systems. In communist Germany, with its militant secularism promoting a Marxist 'freedom from religion', religion seems to function as a remnant from the unenlightened pre-history of the revolution which, for reasons of state, is to be granted only a marginal insitutional existence.[1] In capitalist Germany, with its tolerant secularism promoting a pluralistic 'freedom of religion', religion seems to function as a lawful service system supported by the Church tax for the personal needs of citizens voluntarily associated with the various churches.[2] In the complex world of concretely functioning social relationships, it would appear that the established relationships between churches and states—whether under communism or under capitalism—are very 'worldly' indeed. By this I mean that to the degree that the theory and practice of religion in Germany corresponds to the functional correlations and expectations of a purely secular sociology of religion, to that degree religion fails to embody socially and historically any truly transcendental Mystery. Although the Christian churches continue to engage in liturgical and sacramental ministries, the salt of such celebrations of the coming Kingdom of God loses its savour in so far as its transcendence is not incarnated in the concrete transformations of the personal and social lives of the faithful. The powers of this world have nothing to fear from well integrated comrades or citizens who prefer to spend some time enjoying the songs and rituals of the past. The Christian religion is thereby reduced to aesthetic interludes, symbolic distractions, or ethical exhortations all aimed at reinforcing the integration of the faithful into the demands and functions of secular society. The other-worldly transcendence of the Kingdom of God is at the same time trivialised into private mystifications and (since any genuinely socio-religious expression is repressed) fanaticised into ideologies of unlimited this-wordly progress. The human burdens of social and technological progress are heavy indeed, so the citizens and comrades can safely be permitted small, restorative dosages of 'opium' now and then.

Just as empirical functionalism is increasingly dominant in both Western and Eastern sociologies,[3] so it is not surprising that from this perspective the apparent contradictions between religion in East Germany and West Germany become less and less significant. Church authorities in both Germanies work out elaborate compromises and arrangements with the secular authorities. The sacred is more or less successfully domesticated institutionally by a series of well orchestrated moves designed to preserve the worldly authority of both church and state leaders. Tensions and crises occur, but they can be diplomatically and technically managed. *Plus ça change, plus c'est la meme chose.* Just as the civil authorities in both Germanies jealously guard their respective societies from any dissenting voices, so the ecclesial authorities in both Germanies follow suit. The simple faithful, whether comrade or citizen, must be protected from questioning insights.[4]

To an outsider, therefore, what is really significant about both the practice and theory of religion in Germany today is the unexpected interruptions of this functional predictability of religion in both East and West. Sociologists might term them 'anomalies' and authorities might refer to them as 'fringe' groups or communities. From the viewpoint of the established orders they appear as merely random divergences with little hope of survival or lasting impact upon the supposed long-term stability of social and ecclesial schemes of recurrence. Statistically they seem insignificant, the odds of probability are against them. Rather than withdrawing from social and ecclesial institutions these groups challenge the worldly predictability of those institutions, they interrupt the smooth functioning of bureaucratic expectations by prophetically witnessing to the essential mission of the Church to preach the coming reign of God to the poor, the afflicted, the outcast, and to incarnate the kerygma in its social and ecclesial practice.[5] While such random groups and communities might be sociologically peripheral, many of them are spiritually and theologically very much at the centre of the gospel and the Christian tradition. They have the gracious courage to pray in words and in deeds, to pay the cost of obedient discipleship and the price of a genuine orthodoxy by incarnating their other-worldly faith, hope, and love in personal and social struggles to bring about a more human and free world, through orthopraxis.[6]

If religion is defined only in reference to the social patterns of predictability aimed at stabilising the *status quo*, then these Christians can identify with the 'religionless Christianity' prophesied in the practice and theory of Dietrich Bonhoeffer. It would be mistaken, I believe, to understand these groups as tightly knit, well defined communities whose identity is clearly marked off from the larger numbers of institutionally affiliated Christians. They are not élite nor sectarian. Nor do they fit into the sociological category of charismatic as over against the carriers of a more institutional rationalisation. Their own self-understanding is as varied and diverse as their own personal and social histories. What they share is a growing and deepening realisation that their Christian vocation to follow Christ through his Spirit of repentance, prayer, and compassion interrupts the one-dimensionality of their surrounding successful worlds of state socialism or late capitalism and opens them to the enduring and transformative values of those whose lives, sufferings, and death are not identified with the so-called success stories dominating their worlds. The other-worldly mystery of God narratively communicated in the gospel stories of the coming reign of God opens them to both the transcendentally mystical of the totally Other and the immanently political efforts to realise another social world which would itself foster the values of a responsible openness to, and solidarity with, the myriad victims of history. Responsible openness and solidarity with the victims of history is not the weak-kneed sentimentalism Nietzsche decried in the middle-class Christianity of his day. On the contrary, it is a spiritually strong realisation of how dehumanising and depersonalising secularist and sacralist heroicism in history has been and still is. Because Christian faith is a knowledge born of love, in those whose faith is living and active it sensitises them to how profoundly the heroic projects of a 'humankind on its own' are the bitter fruits of a knowledge born of fear. The victors in history are the heroic élites who use the fear-engendered knowledge in order to oppress and manipulate both nature and their fellow human beings. A faith-inspired knowledge born of love continually goes against the grain of dominative world history, it strives to break the cycles of violence and oppression by disclosing and celebrating the redemptive transformation going on in the other ('under') world of the suffering victims. Only by this practical, other-worldly mysticism will human beings be able to transcend their fears and cease relating to the others as objects for competition and domination. Only by this practical, other-worldly appropriation of the transcendent thrust of the reign of God will humankind become the fully responsible and free political subjects of their destiny on earth.[7]

Although it would be impossible to determine just how numerous Christians with this commitment to the gospel are in Germany, what surprised me during my years of study in West Germany and in my visits to East Germany were the many Christians, both Catholic and evangelical, who were actively and quietly appropriating this type of vocation to the reign of God. They were singularly unimpressed with the rhetoric of Germany's 'economic miracle' (*Wirtschaftswunder*) in both West and East. As an elderly miner in the Ruhr region told me, he had heard that rhetoric during the Third Reich 'and we all know the countless victims that rhetoric futilely tried to hide!' Perhaps it is just because German Christians have experienced the demonic and apocalyptic dimensions of modernity so directly and devastatingly during the last world war and holocaust, that now more and more of them are beginning to hear the gospel's 'repent, the reign of God is at hand' as at once a personal and socio-political summons to go beyond or transcend the banal and deadly functionalisms of economic, political, and ecclesial institutions which regard themselves in practice as ends in and for themselves.

In my opinion it is only against the background of these many histories of suffering as the shadow side of the more strident success histories that one can understand the contemporary projects of German theologians. The task of German theology to mediate reflectively and responsibly the meanings and values of the gospel and the manifold Christian traditions to contemporary socio-cultural situations makes earlier theological challenges seem rather simple by comparison. The mystical, other-worldly dimensions of Christianity can so easily be mystified into a sacralist sectarianism which seeks either the restoration of a new Christendom or an inner emmigration from the concrete concerns and responsibilities of our contemporary world. The social and political this-worldly dimensions of Christianity can so easily be reified into secularist prejudices which reinforce either the one-dimensional bias whereby critical choice must opt for either state socialism or late capitalism, or succumb to a value-neutral pluralism which, in the realm of practical reason, is the correlative of historicism. The various forms of sacralism are the deformations of the mystical severed from the political; the various forms of secularism are the deformations of the political severed from the mystical. Contemporary Germany theologies—like their counterparts in other countries—are faced with the challenge of envisaging new forms of Christian religious theory and practice which preserve the immanent transcendence of the reign of God by going beyond the regressive alternatives of sacralism and secularism.

This task can only be undertaken in the realisation that Germany's own identity crisis is intrinsically related to the identity crisis facing the world as a whole. In so far as late capitalism is a bad materialisation of idealism and state socialism is a bad idealisation of materialism, the division of Germany into two rival socio-economic systems is part of the larger global issues associated with the problems of the North-South or centre-periphery conflicts. Increasingly the really intractable problems of regions and nations are found to be rooted in global problems which do not admit of purely regional or national solutions. To the degree that all forms of idealism and materialism as institutionalised in social relationships are heroic attempts to impose identity constructions on nature and history, to that degree theology must engage in the redemptive criticism of all such identity constructions in the name of the latter's victims. The task of elaborating the constitutive elements of practical reason as reason-not-yet-realised in social reality can only be in any measure successful if that reason-to-be-realised is creatively and critically related to faith as a knowledge born of other (not yet) worldly love. The world to come by the gracious reign of God both transcends all merely human progress and is immanent (*via negationis*) in the suffering victims of that so-called progress. If the scales of human justice are all that we have, if repentence and forgiveness and the justifying love of God is not incarnated in the concrete social relationships of the world, then the cycles of oppression and reprisal will not end until there are no more eyes or teeth left.[8] No merely human justice could ever forgive or redeem the millions upon millions of human beings slaughtered by their fellow human beings just in the past eighty years of our modern and enlightened (*sic!*) twentieth century.[9]

It is in this context that we can understand the efforts of German theologians to engage not only in intra-disciplinary but especially in inter-disciplinary collaboration. If theology is too important to be left only to professionals, it is also too important not to engage, and be engaged by, those involved in serious academic scholarship and science. This is especially so today when the world of our experience 'is in fact a secondary or meta-world, in other words, a world which, in itself and in its deepest reality, bears the deep impression of many systems and theories and which can therefore only be experienced and possibly changed in and through those systems and theories'.[10] There is, for example, a gruesome 'irrationality' in the cool and calculating logic of the nuclear arms race. Technical rationality without wisdom destroys more than it gives life. Yet religious wisdom without science is reduced often to moral generalities incapable of articulating the concrete mediations away from our present irrationalities towards a better and more humane world. One of the ingredients in sublating both a hierarchic sacralist and a bureaucratic secularist authoritarianism is a responsible and creatively critical collaboration between theology and other sciences and scholarships. For religious faith as a knowledge born of love is a constitutive element of any genuinely practical reason, i.e., reason committed to promoting the expansion of effective freedom for all human beings. Authoritarianism of whatever kind is rooted in, and breeds on, fear. The authority of Christian faith is one of service and empowerment. Sacralist superstitions and fears are as inimical to the following of Him who commanded 'Fear not!' as secularist superstitions and fears are inimical to any ongoing realisation of reason in personal and social life. German theologians have historically contributed greatly to meeting the ongoing challenges of critically mediating faith and reason. Their status in West Germany as civil servants offers them not only the opportunities of tax-supported research and writing but also the responsibilities of critically and creatively relating the mystical and political in ways that will transcend the functions of their status by contributing to the imperative tasks of tranforming Church and society.

Notes

1. See *Christianity and Socialism* eds. Johann B. Metz and Jean-Pierre Jossua *Concilium* 105 (1977).
2. See *Christianity and the Bourgeoisie* ed. Johan B. Metz *Concilium* 125 (1979).
3. See Alvin Gouldner *The Coming Crisis of Western Sociology* (New York 1970) pp. 447-477.
4. The repression of critically constructive dissent in East Germany is paralleled by the so-called *Berufsverbot* in West Germany. On the authoritarianist collaboration in East Germay, see Hans-Herman Hücking 'The Christian Life and Church Institutions within the Socialist State' in *Christianity and Socialism* (note 1) 70-73. On similar patterns in West Germany, see Karl Rahner 'Ich Protestiere' *Publik Forum* 23 (16 November 1979) 15-19 and the ongoing controversy on the withdrawal of the *missio canonica* from Prof. Hans Küng, e.g., *Die Welt* 2 January 1980: 'Ratzinger: Kirche schützt die Einfachen vor den Intellektuellen'.
5. See Jürgen Moltmann *The Church in the Power of the Spirit* (New York 1977) pp. 189-196, 337-361. (*Kirche in der Kraft des Geistes* [1975]).
6. See Johann B. Metz *Followers of Christ* (New York 1978) (*Zeit der Orden? Zur Mystik und Politik der Nachfolge* [1977]); also his *Faith in History and Society* (New York 1979), pp. 33-48, 88-153; (*Glaube in Geschichte und Gesellschaft*, [1977]); Hans Küng *On Being a Christian* (New York 1976), pp. 554-602 (*Christ-Sein* [1974]).
7. See Metz *Faith in History and Society*, pp. 32-83; *The Poor and the Church* eds. Norbert Greinacher and Alois Müller *Concilium* 104 (1977); E. Jüngel *Gott als Geheimnis der Welt* (Tübingen 1977).
8. See Matthew Lamb 'The Challenge of Critical Theory' *Sociology and Human Destiny* ed. Gregory Baum (New York 1980) p. 209ff.; Metz *Faith in History and Society* pp. 119-135.
9. See Eugen Kogon, Johann Metz et al. *Gott nach Auschwitz* (Freiburg 1978); also Gil Elliot *Twentieth Century Book of the Dead* (New York 1974).
10. Metz *Faith in History and Society* p. 4; Wolfhart Pannenberg *Theology and the Philosophy of Science* (Philadelphia 1976); (*Wissenschaftstheorie und Theologie* [1973]); and especially, Helmut Peukert *Wissenschaftstheorie-Jandlungstheorie-Fundamentale Theologie* (Frankfurt 1972); *Doing Theology in New Places* eds. Jean-Pierre Jossua and Johann B. Metz *Concilium* 115 (1979).

Malcolm McVeigh

Africa: The Understanding of Religion in African Christian Theologies

THE AFRICAN Church and African theology are increasingly aware of their identity. They are no longer dependent on missionary tutors and Western evangelistic outreach. Africa has come of age theologically, and African Christianity is looking within for new understandings of its faith.

It is a time of flux and ferment but also a time of excitement. Something new is happening, something unique and important. It is not yet fully clear what that something is, but it is becoming clearer. And it is of importance not only for Africa but the world Church.

The Pan-African Conference of Third World Theologians, meeting in Accra, Ghana, 17-23 December 1977, helped to sharpen the issues. Hence the record of that meeting, and especially the 'Final Communiqué', is an important resource for the study of what is happening in African theological thought.

It is still too early to summarise that thought in a word, and perhaps that will always be true. African theology gives every appearance of being a diverse phenomenon. Nevertheless, common themes are emerging that call for attention and consideration.

1. UNITY

One of the common themes dominant in the thought of African theologians today can perhaps best be summed up under the word 'unity'. Unity is a term found throughout the 'Final Communiqué', and its implications are evident at a number of points where the word itself does not appear.

There is, for one thing, an insistence that life itself is a unity and that there can be no separation of existence into sacred and secular categories. 'We affirm that our history is both sacred and secular,' says the document, which then proceeds to call the Church to take seriously this traditional understanding of reality: 'In the traditional setting there was no dichotomy between the sacred and the secular. On the contrary, the sacred was experienced in the context of the secular. This healthy way of understanding our African society must be taken seriously by the Church.'   It is a fact that there is no indigenous word for 'religion' in most African languages. The word *dini*, widely used in East Africa for example, is an Arabic import. A superficial observation might conclude that Africans in traditional society were not religious, which was indeed the conclusion of some early Western observers. A deeper study shows the opposite to be true. Religion has so penetrated every aspect of life that it is impossible to extract it as simply an element of the traditional heritage. To be an African in traditional society is to be a religious person, to have a religious interpretation of life.

African theologians are fully aware of what has taken place due to the impact of Western culture on their common life. They do not reject Christianity, but they are convinced that the Western interpretation of it has produced distortion. They insist that Jesus' approach to life was always 'holistic'.

By their emphasis on 'holism' and their refusal to separate life into sacred and secular categories, African theologians believe that they are able to harmonise African traditional thought with the perspectives of primitive Christianity, thus making an important contribution to the present-day understanding of the Christian gospel outside Africa.

Another aspect of the unity theme is bound up with the African understanding of community. Again African theologians affirm that the traditional culture, with its close-knit society and its concept of the extended family, is closer to the gospel and primitive Christianity than the character of life evident in Western society or its manifestation in the Western churches which first brought the gospel to them.

They do not see the community as suffocating the individual. They believe that there is an important place for the individual in society, but they deny that the individual can ever take precedence over the community: 'God's demand is that human beings be subordinate to God's will for the total human community, making true Christ's command to love our neighbours as we love ourselves. Love for us signifies a communal act of obedience to God who is eternally with us.'

It is also in this light that one must see the strong reaction in the 'Final Communiqué' against all forms of sexism and racism and the particular understanding of African theology relative to 'ethnicity' (the document never uses the word 'tribalism'). The inherent differences between people are not the problem. It is what is done with those differences that causes disruption: 'Ethnicity in Africa, as anywhere in the world, must not be confused with racism. Ethnicity is a positive element in any society. It can, however, be misused by outside powers to serve the ends of racism and cause disunity, wars and human suffering.'

In yet another way, the African understanding of community includes right relations between the living and those who have gone before, those sometimes called 'the living dead'. One of the tasks facing African theology today is to address itself to a reformulation of the concerns of the traditional ancestor cult in a way meaningful for the Christian understanding of the communion of the saints.

The ferment presently going on in African theology cannot be understood unless one sees it within the context of a world view that recognises the reality of both the seen and unseen worlds. African theology insists that there is no place in Africa for a purely materialist interpretation of existence. Rather, Africans affirm the unity between the two worlds and the importance of understanding the relationship between them.

2. CONTINUITY

A second term which may be used to describe the present ferment in African theology is the word 'continuity'. This theme (and the ideas which surround it) has two principal focal points.

There is, first of all, the question of continuity with the traditional African heritage. African theologians are not calling for a return to the past, but they are asking that the past be taken seriously, especially as past and present meet in the reality of today's Africa. As sources for present-day theology, the 'Final Communiqué' lists African anthropology, African traditional religions and African independent churches. What does this mean?

African theologians are aware that the concerns of traditional religions must be addressed if the gospel is to speak meaningfully to the present situation. Perhaps it was only to be expected, but the mission churches have to date been overly preoccupied with Western problems and too little interested in those distinctively relevant to Africa. One of the reasons that African theology finds the independent churches so important is that it perceives those churches to have gone further than the mission churches in bringing to bear the Christian faith as an answer to traditional problems. Obviously, all peoples share many similar questions, but the mode of their expression and the solutions which are meaningful to them differ according to circumstance. African theologians are increasingly aware of this difference. They know that the gospel has resources that speak directly to their situation, and they see their task as one of opening channels for those resources to play their role. Nevertheless, one ought not to see African traditional religions simply as a source for questions. There are also answers coming from traditional Africa of permanent value, indeed a spiritual interpretation of life which can enrich all peoples and contribute to a deeper understanding of the Christian gospel itself.

Continuity with the traditional African heritage is important for African theology, but continuity with the historic Christian faith is also vital. There is no evidence in the 'Final Communiqué' of an attempt to remove African theology from the Christian context. African theology rather will be Christian theology in an African context. This is manifest from beginning to end in the document. The first words of the introduction are: 'We are African Christians', and allegiance to Jesus Christ as Lord and Saviour is affirmed immediately afterward: 'We came together because of our deep concern for faith in Jesus Christ in Africa. It is this faith in the Lord of history that speaks to us concretely today. As we joyfully praise the saving Lord and share our problems, we are aware of the very real presence of the incarnate Jesus who comforts us and gives us hope.' Faith in Jesus Christ is the foundation stone of the document, and continuity with the historic Christian faith comes to expression in various ways.

A deep esteem for the Scriptures appears everywhere: 'The Bible is the basic source of African theology because it is the primary witness of God's revelation in Jesus Christ. No theology can retain its Christian identity apart from scripture.' In the conclusion of the 'Final Communiqué', 'a return to the Scriptures' is credited as the principal resource for the renewal of the churches.

Still another aspect of this continuity is the clear affirmation that 'African Christianity is a part of worldwide Christianity'. African theologians are seeking new ways to speak relevantly to the African situation, but they do not see this as being accomplished in isolation from either the past history of the Church or the present diversity of the faith's expression in different parts of the world: 'The Christian heritage is also important for African theology. This is the heritage of the life and history of the Church since the time of our Lord.' Furthermore, the document specifically calls for 'dialogue with non-African theologies'.

How does one bridge the gap between past and present as it relates to both the traditional African heritage and the historic Christian faith? That is, how does one create a continuity between these two continuities? African theologians find that question important. Basically, they see 'the inherent values in the traditional religions' as 'a preparation for the gospel'. But they are also convinced that 'the beliefs and practices of the traditional religions in Africa can enrich Christian theology and spirituality'.

The contribution of the African independent churches to the life of African Christianity and African theology is to be seen in this context. As noted above, the independent churches have generally taken African culture more seriously than their misssion Church counterparts. And they have in many cases gone further in their adaptation of the Christian faith to the African milieu. Hence not only their practices but also their thought are a source of great importance for African theology.

3. LIBERATION

It is not possible to understand the present ferment within African theology without some mention of the word 'liberation'. African theologians are greatly preoccupied with its meaning, and in fact the word itself is widely used in the 'Final Communiqué'.

A superficial reading of that document might lead one to conclude that African theology is simply liberation theology cast in the mould of Latin America or black theology in the U.S.A. That would be a misreading of the situation. African theology, to be sure, is cognizant of what is going on in the theological thought of Latin America and among blacks in the U.S.A., and it finds many points of contact with them from within the African situation.

African theologians have a deep empathy for persons facing any kind of oppression. They too have experienced the reality of dehumanisation under colonialism. Nor is the problem merely colonialism in the past. They see neo-colonialism at work in their present situation, and they are fully aware of the continued existence of overt colonialism in Southern Africa.

Nevertheless, it is important to recognise that the focus on liberation in African theology is not confined to political, social and economic conditions. The 'Final Communiqué' does not perhaps express this as clearly as it appears in some of the other papers read at the conference. There was considerable discussion of this question in Accra. Still, the strong emphasis given in the 'Final Communiqué' to the place of African anthropology, African traditional religions and African independent churches, for whom political, social and economic issues in the modern sense are not a major consideration, suggests that something more is involved in the African understanding of liberation.

African traditional religions are basically preoccupied with the problem of evil in a different way: fears concerning witchcraft, concerns for right relations with ancestral spirits, sickness and misfortune, the daily tragedies of life. A major purpose of these religions is to reverse the direction, to turn misfortune into fortune and failure into success, to bring healing and wholeness to life. African independent churches seek to accomplish the same ends, healing and wholeness, through the use of Christian resources.

There is a sense in which one can describe the present ferment in African theology within the context of the liberation theme, namely salvation as liberation. And three streams are pouring into the cauldron. One stream comes from missionary Christianity and identifies salvation as liberation from sin. Another stream comes from liberation theology cast in the Latin American mould, which understands salvation as liberation from oppressive political, social and economic conditions. Still a third stream comes from traditional Africa and sees salvation as liberation from the objective forces of evil that lie behind sickness and misfortune and the daily tragedies of life.

African theologians may differ in assessing their relative significance, but it is obvious that all play a role in present-day African theological thought and, significantly, in Scripture as well. Jesus was concerned about the forgiveness of sins but also the healing of disease and the liberation of the poor and oppressed. Indeed, African theology may be the first to forge a meaningful synthesis of the three.

African theology is very much alive and active. It is a time of excitement and ferment. The new is emerging, ideas and perspectives that will enrich not only Africa and the African Church but world Christianity. The Church universal will do well to follow the debate.

PART IV
Bulletins

Italo Mancini

Philosophy of Religion

IT IS easy enough to understand why it is so difficult to give a complete picture of the state of this discipline, which is increasingly becoming the centre of attention. If we merely give a list of names, works, schools, etc., we run the risk of becoming bogged down in a morass of data. If on the other hand we turn directly to the problems themselves, then we run the risk of over-emphasising our personal point of view. I will try to resolve this dilemma by choosing the latter course but not neglecting important names and works and the useful aid of bibliography. This is all the more essential in this discipline which began as the very heart of philosophy, even though it has now become distinct from it, with Spinoza (*Tractatus theologico-politicus* 1670), Kant (*Die Religion innerhalb der Grenzen der blossen Vernunft* 1793) and Hegel (*Die Philosophie der Geschichte*). During this century this discipline developed a method and its own specific foundations which have given rise to large interpretative hypotheses, so that we have the phenomenological, the idealist, the existentialist, the Marxist, the psychoanalytic form of philosophy of religion and so on. On the basis of what I have written about this discipline, for which I think I have given sound historical and theoretical reasons, I should like to pick out certain questions to discuss rather than make pronouncements on. I should like to ascertain what in these questions remains antagonistic to philosophy of religion and what is outside its scope.

1. WHY A PHILOSOPHY OF RELIGION?

I want to go beyond the two opposing justifications of philosophy of religion, namely, to defend religion (apologetics) or to condemn it (atheism). These are extrinsic and ideological procedures in the negative sense because they do not seek truth but rather domination (the Nicene 'hold as true' rather than 'true'[1]). I also want to go beyond idealist constructivism (religion as a 'province'[2] of the transcendental spirit: Schleiermacher) and phenomenology which tries 'simply' to describe the phenomenon in detail, which of course runs into the difficulty strongly felt by van de Leeuw[3]: How to describe what is by its nature indescribable. I want to go beyond the researches on the sacred, which in the massive work of Mircea Eliade at least, ended by being an enquiry into the basis of being and is extremely suggestive on the relation between the sacred and profane.[4] Beyond all this, which I regard as philosophical considerations on religion, if we take religion in the strong sense as (to quote Dilthey)[5] 'enormous masses of religious life' present in history and human experience, presumed to be revealed or given by God, which re-establishes the object of the philosophy of religion within theology, and if we take philosophy of religion as a *critical consciousness of theology*, I think that a good way of looking at philosophy of religion is that upheld and defended by Kant, who in this was a disciple of Rousseau.

Kant holds that the philosopher has the right to ask not only what in religion can be reached by 'simple' reason, as he did in *Die Religion innerhalb der Grenzen de blossen Vernunft*[6] but also that the philosopher has the right to decide on the reasonableness and 'attractiveness'[7] of Christianity and this he did in his *Der Streit der Fabuttäten*. This Kant holds even if, as Karl Barth observes,[8] by wanting to give (*Formwille*) a human and anthropocentric form to the content of theology he is often unfaithful to it in his conception of evil, the Son of God and the redemption of the Church. Kant defends this intervention and this requirement of reason on two fundamental grounds. First, because he thinks that religion should be tested by reason, not the complicated and technical reason of critical theory, but simple common reason, which is shared by all (Rousseau's Savoy priest's reason), so that such a great gift as salvation can be shared by all and that this sovereign good should finally be the goal of moral reason. Without this sharing based on common reason belonging to all, conscious salvation would be available only to the few, and this would produce discrimination and false spiritual heights. In the language of the pharmacy of his time, Kant says that reason functions as a 'vehicle'[9] or medium to conduct the active elements.

Kant's second ground was that anyone deprived of the instrument of reason is in danger of falling into fanaticism. In the first pages of *Die Religion* he observes that a religion would not last long if it did not accord with reason. And in a letter to Staudlin[10] he says that the theologian's decisive weapon must be persuasion or consent, otherwise there remains nothing but violence. Consent or violence are the alternatives Kant sees, and this is why he thinks that religion should be open to reason.

2. THE CONUNDRUM OF PHILOSOPHY OF RELIGION

These reasons for a philosophy of religion, which are political, because they demand a religion accessible to all who share common reason (*Allgemeinvernunft*), and for a religion communicated by conviction rather than by violence to human dignity through force (carrot or stick) are important. But they are not the only ones. There is the need for philosophical inquiry, to make sense of religion. Otherwise philosophy of religion would be reduced to gnosis and well known forms of religious philosophy (Blondel, the endless forms of spiritualism). Even without a complete definition of the concept of religion, we can say in advance that it will involve a necrotic weakening in this area of rationalisation and determination. The biblical sense of religious experience stresses exactly the opposite view to that supported by Kant. It stresses election (as against common reason), the radical break and paradox (as against rational continuity). Kierkegaard noted in a page of his diary,[11] that rational investigation belonged to philosophical discourse, whereas the distinctive characteristic of the Christian is the paradox. This is what Pascal called a wager (*pari*)[12] and Lucien Goldmann called faith[13] and what he sees as the centre of the systems of Augustine, Pascal, Kant and even Marx.

I should like to give a few examples showing how the *meaning* of Christianity resists philosophical inquiry. First, God's absolute sovereignty, as conceived by the metaphysician by the farthest stretch of his reason cannot be reconciled with the biblical God's scandalous and amazing behaviour. As Bonhoeffer says in his letters from prison,[14] this God chose impotence, the Cross and emptying himself by taking human form. If philosophy's highest achievement is to speak about God, religion's minimum is to be able to speak *with* God and this can only happen on God's initiative. Thus, here the meaning of religion is at odds with reason. Only the paradox makes sense of it. Can existing for others, which we find as the definition of the biblical God and which represents the true 'exodus' from the Zeusian forms of the Most High, before whom 'the servant stands dry-mouthed',[15] be called identical with the metaphysicians' necessary being, blind to the human condition,[16] whereas in the Bible God takes the form of the oppressed?

Second example: the Platonic idea of the natural immortality of man goes against the biblical concept of the resurrection of the flesh, which requires that victory over the 'last enemy', death, should be a supreme effect of grace. This is not a natural continuity as with Bloch's 'hand' and 'glove', the latter being the body and the former the soul, so that the hand can take off the glove and still survive.[17]

Thus there is a sense of religion and faith which transcends and almost mocks[18] philosophical inquiry. Faith has its reason which reason does not know.[19] And of course philosophy also has its reasons, and in the field of faith it meets absurdity, as Harnack's 'scientific theology' showed over against Barth's one and only kerygmatic theology. Against what appeared to be an 'arrogant dualist gnosticism'[20] Harnack rightly observed that this would mean 'consigning to barbarism' all human culture, that Kant and Goethe should be considered atheists, that there can be no education for faith, and that even love of our neighbour cannot be connected with love of God.

How can we reconcile these two requirements, which are both legitimate and totally opposed? Not by champing religion between the teeth of philosophy. Maritain wrote: 'A cherry between our teeth contains more mystery than the whole of idealist philosophy.'[21] This way is a false reconciiation known as 'reductionism' or a 'bourgeois' form of Christianity.[22] It is also impracticable to go the way of kerygmatic surrealism, which denies any kind of continuity and gives over to death all man's being, having and doing, so that the message is brought by a man as a mere 'occasion' in the way a dog brings a good piece of meat in his mouth.

3. THE UTOPIA OF PHILOSOPHY OF RELIGION

So what is to be done? If we are not trying to make a religious philosophy or a theology which is pure proclamation, we must try for a philosophy *of* religion, in which philosophy investigates religion without ever trying totally to resolve it into a gnosis. spiritualism or metaphysic. This could be called the *Utopia* of philosophy of religion. Utopia in the sense that the concept is never adequate to the reality it is trying to define (word, event, community, commandment). Adorno extended this to all knowledge. He speaks of a negative dialectic in which no subject is ever identical with its predicate. 'The Utopia of knowledge,' he says, 'would mean opening up the aconceptual with concepts without ever identifying them.'[23]

If this is true it means that the Utopia of the philosophy of religion is a deuteronomic knowledge, that is to say a knowledge which arises as a consequence of a 'divine *a priori*'[24] in the logical and ontological sense. It is based more on the logic of recognition (hence the epistemological primacy of the hermeneutic) that on pure thought (for some this means the end of metaphysics, but I do not agree; metaphysics can offer a schema for the possibility of religious fact). It has the same structure as the 'humanities' (*Geisteswissenschaften*) which are based more on evaluation than absolute propositions.

Thus the philosophy of religion does not begin and end with a single philosophical act, the identification of the 'immense object'[25] which proves to be 'an impossible'[26] when confronted with human possibilities, aesthetic, moral, metaphysical, political. It encircles its object, as it were besieging it. To determine what these philosophical acts are is the question of method. Three are inescapable. First, to determine what is the specific object of the concept of religion. This does not include consideration of natural religion. Second, to decide in what way and within what limits the truth of religion can be tested (I would put it: How does it come about that a religion can become my faith?) Third, since religion is a doctrine of salvation and therefore lasts as long as there is something in distress[27] which needs saving, its link with the practical must be established and it must be compared with other great hypotheses of liberation, such as cybernetics, semeiotics, psychoanalysis, and above all Marxism.

There are therefore two main questions for a philosophy of religion: its truth and its efficacity, its value and its use. Because of the necessary link between theory and practice these two questions are one and mean the same thing. However, the final justification is not theoretical but practical, not the vision but the capacity to liberate. Kant was right when he said that in religion 'everything depends on the doing'.[28]

We cannot say more here about what kind of philosophy religion can sustain without being reduced to something else. I think it is very important that theory carries over into a practical challenge, even though the question of its saving power and efficacy in liberating mankind remains continually an open one.

Notes

1. Friedrich Nietzsche *Frammenti posumi 1887-1888* (Milan 1971) p. 14.
2. Schleiermacher *U'ber die Religion* (Hamburg 1961) p. 20.
3. Gerardus van der Leeuw *Fenomenologia della religione* (Turin 1960) (epilogue).
4. Mircea Eliade *Il sacro e il profano* (Turin 1967). For a useful synthesis of Eliade's thought, see Ioan Culianu *Mircea Eliade* (Assisi 1978).
5. W. Dilthey *Das Problem der Religion* in *Ges. Schr.* VI, p. 288.
6. Italo Mancini *Kant e la teologia* (Assisi 1975).
7. Kant *Das Ende aller Dinge* in AK VIII, p. 338.
8. Karl Barth *Die protestantische Theologie im 19. Jahrhundert* (Hamburg 1975) I, pp. 221-258.
9. Kant *Die Religion innerhalb der Grenzen der blossen Vernunft* (Hamburg 1956) p. 117.
10. Letter of 4 May 1773 in AK XI, p. 249.
11. Kierkegaard *Diario* ed. Cornelio Fabro (Brescia 1948) I p. 138.
12. Blaise Pascal *Pensées et opuscules* ed. Leon Brunschvicg (Paris 1946) pp. 435-442 (no. 233).
13. Lucien Goldmann *Il dio nascosto. La visione tragica in Pascal e Racine* (Bari 1971) pp. 15-38.
14. Dietrich Bonhoeffer *Widerstand und Ergebung* (Munich 1964) pp. 242, 246.
15. Ernst Bloch *Atheismus im Christentum* (Frankruft a. M. 1968) p. 54.
16. Italo Mancini 'Dio è nero?' in *Futuro dell'uomo e spazio per l'invocazione* (Ancona 1975) pp. 107-118.
17. Ernst Bloch *Religione in eredita* (Brescia 1979) p. 94.
18. See Acts 17:32.
19. Pascal *Pensées* pp. 458-459 (nos. 277, 278, 279).
20. Karl Barth *Der Römerbrief* (Zurich 1976) p. 60.
21. Jacques Maritain *Les Degrees du savoir* (Paris 1958) p. 666.
22. Italo Mancini 'La grande età del cristianesimo borghese e la sua irrealizzazione', preface to Karl Barth *La teologia protestante nel secolo decimonono* (Milan 1979) pp. 9-60.
23. Theodor W. Adorno *Dialettica negativa* (Turin 1970) p. 9.

24. Barth *Der Römerbrief* p. 268.
25. G. W. F. Hegel *Vorlesungen über die Philosophie der Religion* (Hamburg 1966) I p. 287.
26. Barth *Der Römerbrief* pp. 90-120.
27. This, I think, is Marx's thesis in *Zur Judenfruse*.
28. Kant *Der Streit der Fakultäten* in AK VII, p. 41.

Victor Turner

Religion in Current Cultural Anthropology

WESTERN anthropologists eschew formal definition of religion and focus on religious conduct: ritual and religious organisation. Geertz writes representatively (1968:1): 'The comparative study of religion has always been plagued by this peculiar embarrassment: the elusiveness of its subject matter. The problem is not one of constructing definitions of religion. We have had quite enough of those; their very number is a symptom of our malaise. It is a matter of discovering just what sorts of beliefs and practices support what sorts of faith under what sorts of conditions.' This pragmatic outlook avoids direct inquiry into the ultimate roots of the faith of an individual or community, preferring to concentrate on how 'it is sustained in this world by symbolic forms and social arrangements' (Geertz, *op. cit.* 2). The title of a series of books published by Cornell University Press and edited by V. Turner exemplifies this approach: *Symbol, Myth and Ritual*. Turner defined ritual as 'formal behaviour for occasions not given over to technological routine, having reference to beliefs in mystical beings or powers' (1967:19), a definition clearly influenced by the legacy of confluent positivism, materialism, and rationalism represented by the scholarly chain of Comte, Feuerbach, Durkheim, and, more recently in Britain, Balinowski and Radcliffe-Brown.

Shakespeare wrote that sometimes 'by indirections we find directions out'. The focus on ritual, in so far as ritual was regarded as processual in essence rather than rubrical, performance rather than competence (Hymes 1974:130-131), and composed of 'structures of experience' rather than to be explained by cognitive structures abstracted from human beings and their conduct, has generated several studies which return anthropology to the problem of religion in relation not only to social but also to personal experience. One source of this renewal has been Arnold van Gennep's epoch-making book, *Les Rites de Passage* (1909), which grouped together all rituals 'that accompany transitions from one situation to another and from one cosmic or social world to another' (p. 13). He divided these *rites of passage* or transitional rituals, into rites of separation, threshold rites, and rites of re-aggregation, for which he also uses the terms preliminal, liminal, and postliminal. While van Gennep often insisted upon the importance of the central, 'liminal' stage, he did not probe its characteristics in any depth. Nor did he study the total system of *rites de passage* in a single culture, nor the engagement of such a system with the ongoing social process in a single sociocultural system. His achievement was the elicitation of a common processual form from a tangled mass of cross-cultural ritual data. But he was occupied with other important matters: the establishment of folklore and what is now called folklife studies on a sound scientific basis. He should be honoured for leaving anthropology a clue to a deeper understanding of the human condition than has been provided by functionalism, structuralism, or dialectical materialism (a paradoxical phrase, for how can matter be 'dialectical', since this would imply 'anti-matter' as a term in the process?).

The clue is 'liminality', which has many implications when it is directly related to crucial phases of human experience. For in protracted rituals of any complexity in innumerable cultures the liminal phase implies the termination or suspension of cultural classifications and social status-roles and the rules and sanctions which define and uphold them. What formerly 'mattered' matters no more, what will matter is being generated in the domain of liminal seclusion set apart from the mundane, quotidian world. It would not be a rash generalisation to state that in prolonged liminal phases, and particularly in initiation rituals from childhood to adulthood, symbolic objects and activities represent in their most general aspect, not only metaphorical (and metanymic) birth and death, but also a transient state in which these (and other) opposites of quotidian experience become one. Caves, tunnels, seclusion huts or camps, may represent simultaneously tombs (of former social-structural selves) and wombs (of new identities). Liminality itself is a process; in certain of its phases symbolic objects, roles, activities, and relationships represent the coincidence of quotidian opposites or non-duality. Liminaries, whether they be initiands or initiators may be regarded as hermaphroditic or theriomorphic. In other phases, initiands may be treated and symbolised as without attributes or qualities as these are defined in the 'normal' or 'secular' domain. On the other hand, in some liminal situations and phases axiomatic cultural values may be exhibited to the novices, often as multivocal symbols, which may themselves be explained in gnomic or obscure language. In life-crisis rituals or in rituals of induction into secret societies, the liminal stage may often be held in sequestered or concealed sites; while calendrical and seasonal rituals are distinguished by public, open liminal periods, containing episodes of ribaldry and play, and characterised by a 'surplus of signifiers'. *Per contra*, the central symbols of ritual initiations are often few in number, though manifold in meaning. Again, the public liminality of rituals organised in terms of annual, astronomical or liturgical cycles may contain many symbolic reversals: of status, gender, age, caste, ethnicity, temporal order, etc.

Since structuralists (Jakobson and Lévi-Strauss) and semioticians (R. Barthes, U. Eco, and others) have drawn liberally on language to elucidate cultural processes, phenomena, and relationships (sometimes perhaps without recognising that the technical vocabulary of one discipline usually becomes metaphor or analogue when applied to the data of another—though sometimes with illuminating heuristic consequences), perhaps I may be permitted to speculate that cultural processes, like verbs, have different 'moods'. Much of liminality may be said to be in culture's 'subjunctive' or 'optative' moods, since many of its phenomena express desire, supposition, hypothesis, and possibility rather than state an 'actual fact', according to the given culture's standard definition of 'factuality', 'reality', or 'actuality'. It is the mood of 'may be', 'might be', 'the possibility of being' (like Rainer Maria Rilke's 'unicorn'!), the mood of 'if I *were* you', or of 'as-if it were'. The indicative mood controls the quotidian areas of economic activity, much of law and politics, and much of domestic life. The term expresses an act, state, or occurrence as 'actual'. In a specific instance of ritual, some components are 'indicative', having to do with the organisation of events, the construction of shrines, the demarcation of celebratory space from ordinary territory, etc. These and similar activities produce a 'frame', within which the subjunctive domain is privileged to exist. This is the world of the exhibition of *sacra*, symbols of a higher reality; of the dramatisation of creation narratives; of the appearance, in many initiation rituals seen cross-culturally, of masked and monstrous figures; of the construction of complicated shrines which may, as in Bali, represent a cosmological hierarchy of beings; of the revelation, in mid-liminality, of figurines and wall-paintings used to instruct and catechise naked, painted, or uniformed novices undergoing initiatory transformation. One might say that there are not only rigid and rule-bounded activities and the display of symbolic objects held to be of high antiquity and great sacredness, but also liminal units of space-time in which improvisation and spontaneity may be mandatory. In liminality new construals of ancient symbols may be made; there may be a *play* of ideas and a rearranging of symbols as well as the resolemnisation and reconsecration of symbolic archetypes. In other words, there may be some scope for *reflexivity* in the subjunctive domain. In their life-crisis rituals, in their healing rites, in their calendrical ceremonies, members of a community may subject themselves and their presentational symbols to keen self-scrutiny, being at once subject and direct object. Actual conduct may be compared with the paradigmatic deeds of divinities, saviours, saints and culture heroes. Or new ways of modelling or framing social life may be proposed and sometimes legitimated in the very heat of liminal performance, perhaps in the hyperaroused states associated with shamanism, spirit-possession, trance, etc., but often as a kind of mentifact of popular creativeness in the public liminality of great cyclical rituals.

As counterpoint to the cultural elaboration found in liminality stands its social structural simplicity. Between incumbents of positions in 'secular' politico-jural systems there exist intricate and situationally shifting networks of rights and duties proportioned to their rank, status, and corporate affiliation. In the liminal period such distinctions and gradations tend to be eliminated. A structure of a very simple kind emerges: a class of initiators collectively exerts complete authority over a class of initiands: among the latter there is often complete equality of 'non-status' (Turner 1967:99). The initiands confront one another, as it were, integrally and not in compartmentalised fashion as incumbents of structural positions and players of roles. Turner has called this modality of human interrelatedness *communitas* (1969:123), comparing it with Buber's notions of *I-Thou* and *Essential We* (1961:51). Typically it is ephemeral as *experience* but capable of generating far-reaching cultural and social consequences.

How, then, does the comparative study of ritual processes viewed as crucial 'moments' in the lives both of persons and communities, assist us in the study of religion? One answer is that they provide us with a set of 'frames' in which we can obtain information, like the traces left by the Brownian movement of electrons in a mist chamber, about modalities of experience which normally escape the nets of cognitive theorising and quotidian observation. Jakob Boehme once wrote: 'In Yea and Nay all things consist'—and in centrally liminal ritual phenomena and processes we may sometimes glimpse the visible shadow of that invisible 'Nay'—counterstroke to all 'positive', 'structural' assertions. Rappaport expresses a similar notion (1979:205): 'In the liturgical sign, which is multivocalic and bipolar, which may be at once iconic, indexical, and denotative, and which is embodied in something substantial—a cross, a flag, a posture—there seems to be union of a concatenated mass of simple significations into a single but complex representation. Once such a representation is brought into being it may be treated as *being* (author's italics) what is symbolised.' A Catholic must think here of the hyperliminal moment of the Eucharistic elevation when bread is transubstantiated into Host whose consumption converts parishioners of diverse social structural attributes into the single Mystical Body of the Church, and a moment of pure existential *communitas* is realised.

Positivism does not admit that there is a liminal 'Nay'. It would have all in the cultural indicative mood. The subjunctive mood, which is to be considered as a font or 'abyss' of possibilities rather than the mere lack or opposite of some positive character or quality, would be considered by it—if it considered religious and aesthetic phenomena with any degree of seriousness— as 'fantasy', the cultural equivalent of 'primary process' thinking, generative only of superstitious notions and fetishistical activities. Similarly, from this standpoint, human sociality is exhausted by the notion of 'social structure', the 'more or less distinctive arrangement of specialised and mutually dependent institutions and the institutional organisations of positions and/or actors which they imply, all the durable parts of the structure being functionally interconnected so as to preserve the general form of the whole'. *Communitas*, from the 'positive' standpoint, must be regarded as '*anti*-structure', since it abolishes status distinctions and in general reunites what social structure and cultural taxonomies have pulled apart.

But if the liminal phase in ritual—and in the numerous paraliminal performative genres, including theatre, carnival, ballet, concerts of music, and narrative modes, such as myth, folk epic, literary epic, the novel, etc., which may be regarded as ultimately derived from ritual or at least numbered among its 'dialectical dancing partners' (Grimes 1977)—'carries' central messages of the religions served by their rituals, and if ritual is no mere 'reflection' or 'expression' (in however 'disguised' or 'oblique' a form) of social structure, then we may find in it clues to the nature of religion not readily available to abstract, decontextualised thought. *Communitas* in ritual, even if it be only 'symbolic' or 'normative' *communitas* rather than spontaneous *communitas*, reveals 'social structure' to be a fabrication, a noble or ignobile 'lie', a 'social construction of reality', while it is antistructure that is the 'reality'. We must reverse our signs: the liminal 'Nay' is revealed as a religious affirmation. Indeed, social and cognitive structures may now perhaps be seen as residues of liminal experience, the spent husks of growth processes, formalised markers of moments of significant transition in the lives of groups and persons. This is not to declare them to be impediments to further culturally generative experiences. As sources of limitation and constraint they provide demarcated channels through which new currents of thought, feeling and desire may flow. They also provide a lexicon and grammar of symbols and words whereby we may communicate, but this very language 'competence' (in Chomskyan parlance) creates distinctions which, as Rappaport writes (1979:206), 'cut the world into bits—into categories, classes, oppositions, and contrasts'. At the heart of liminality, its sacred heart in vitalising rituals, sometimes betokened by a sacrificial act of self-abandonment, is the salve for this dismemberment of the unitary human image. It is infinite in possibility, the source of power and might. Among the Peoples of the Book it is symbolised and personified as God: in much of South and East Asia it is the Way without attributes. It may be thought of as First Cause or Still Centre. Or its infinite modalities may be personified in a polytheistic pantheon. The ritual process reveals that religion (from *religare*, to bind back) re-binds by unbinding (from social structure), for the course of unity (or non-duality) is in anti-structure, though it generates and sustains the multitudinous structures of nature, mind, and culture till they fetter humankind. Then it dissolves or destroys them.

Bibliography

Buber, M. *Between Man and Man* trans. R. G. Smith (London and Glasgow 1961).
Geertz, C. *Islam Observed* (New Haven and London 1968).
Gennep, A. van *Les Rites de Passage* (Paris 1909).
Grimes, R. 'Ritual and Drama' Unpublished Ms. (1977).
Hymes, D. *Foundations in Sociolinguistics: An Ethnographic Approach* (Philadelphia 1979).
Rappaport, R. A. *Ecology, Meaning and Religion* (Richmond, California 1979).
Turner, V. *The Forest of Symbols: Aspects of Ndembu Ritual* (Ithaca and London 1967).
Turner, V. *The Ritual Process: Structure and Anti-Structure* (Chicago 1969).

Natale Terrin

On the Definition of Religion in the History of Religions

THE DEFINITION of religion is strictly related to the problem of method in historico-religious studies; basically what one is dealing with is a particular case of the very close correlation which exists in every discipline between the definition/comprehension of the object and the methodological framework that derives from it.

The present state of studies in the field of the 'history of the religions'[1] demonstrates the truth of this and shows very clearly that the rethinking of the method of study which is going on in this field today is fully reflected in the growing problem surrounding the object 'religion'. This problem is apparent in the ever-increasing difficulty people have in achieving genuine possession of such 'religion' via some kind of appropriate definition, description, conception or understanding.[2]

It is therefore important that the history of religions should continue to concentrate on, to be concerned about its object, in so far as searching for a definition of religion means bringing under review the classic methodological problems, such as, for example, the problem of *a priori* or reductionist thinking in the religious field, the problem of the possibility or otherwise of evaluative descriptions and understanding, of the legitimacy or otherwise of an essential and/or normative definition, the problem of the significance of the autonomy and the specificity of religion, and, finally, of the social function it assumes.

In this context the attempt to define religion is by no means an academic exercise, or one that gives merely aesthetic pleasure. It is, on the contrary, of vital importance, above all for the historian of religion, who should be familiar with the particular range of his field of research, and, secondly, because every definition as at once *symptomatic* and *directional*: it implies, in fact, a precise sensibility, while leading at the same time to a choice in the process of solving the problems listed above.

Having thus outlined the general problems involved in the definition of religion, I will limit myself here to showing how various schools and trends in the history of religion are associated with different definitions of religion, and secondarily, to demonstrating that the defining of religion is never a naïve, unsophisticated occupation, but is rather the result of a choice which frequently tends to be expressed practically as a wager about the validity of a given methodological perspective.

For the sake of simplicity and greater clarity, I will present here a number of definitions of religion and the relative problems surrounding them, mentioning by name only a few of the better known schools and trends and, within these schools and trends selecting a few representative names. Naturally a certain amount of simplification and approximation is necessary, for which I beg the indulgence of the reader.

1. THE HISTORICO-POSITIVE TREND IN EUROPE

The first great trend in the study of the history of the religions, which is connected with a particular form of religious adherence and a determined attempt to encompass 'religion' as a phenomenon, is represented today by a number of eminent European scholars, amongst whom the most qualified are the Italian U. Bianchi and the German K. Rudolph, followers, respectively of R. Pettazzoni and W. Baetke.

The approach to the study of religion followed by this historico-positive trend, together with the specific connected problem of defining religion, has frequently been discussed by U. Bianchi, to whom I will therefore make particular reference in the course of these brief notes.

It should be noted first of all that the specific aim of the Italian author is to maintain confidence in positive inquiry, on the basis of which every previous definition of religion must inevitably be questioned. Rightly emphasising the conundrum intrinsic to all historico-religious research, according to which, on the one hand, the historico-positive study should itself form the religious concept and, on the other, such a study should necessarily presuppose some kind of definition of the object before research can be undertaken, the author argues that every conceivable definition of religion should depart from a twofold base: the concept of religion inherent in what, in one's own culture, is called 'religion'—an essential element to enable the research to get off the ground; and secondly—decisively—the actual historical research. Only within a framework in which the definition of religion is measured continually against the progress that results from historical knowledge of the object will one arrive at a definition which is not a prioristic, and therefore not ideological. Religion will emerge, therefore, as 'an analogy' or as 'an historical universal', in other words '. . . it will appear as a family of phenomena, which, however diverse and irreducible, will nevertheless manifest, if not always a continuity and a real connection in a proven acknowledged historical sequence, at least a partial affinity or "analogy" . . . of character, content and function'.[3] Strictly speaking, therefore, what is provided is not a genuine definition of religion, but only a definition *in fieri* which is gradually being formed in close conjunction with history and with the attention paid to the analogies and affinities which, from time to time, permit us to speak of something as 'religion'.

It is obvious that in this context every definition of religion is suspect, in so far as it could cast doubt on or totally invalidate historico-positive research through the more or less disguised introduction of *a priori* and reductionist ideas which have nothing to do with the reality of history. Bianchi is very definite on this point, both in connection with psychological and sociological definitions, and in connection with the definitions—in his view blatantly reductionist—of the religionists.[4]

Many scholars agree substantially with such a characterisation of religion within the context of historico-religious studies, and with the methodological positions that result from it, among them A. Brelich, G. Lanczkowski, N. Ringgren, Z. Weblowski, G. Widengren and—as already mentioned above—K. Rudolph.

I should like to make one point in connection with the last-named author. The historico-positive method seeks to maintain before its object that ideal distance which makes objectivity possible in such a way that the ideas of the researcher do not become confused with the historical facts and the reality in which religion is incarnated. Bianchi writes that the historian of religions *qua* historian 'should be neither a believer nor a non-believer'.[5] Recently, however, K. Rudolph abandoned this principle, suggesting that religion should be studied as a form of ideology, and that the history of religions (*Religionswissenschaft*) should be understood as a 'critique of the religious ideology'.[6] The new thesis of the German historian provides food for thought. Is it an isolated case, or is it an example of a fairly recurrent temptation met with by those who strive for so-called 'objectivity' of historico-positive research?

2. THE MARBURG SCHOOL

At the opposite extreme from the objectivity of historico-positive research is the Marburg school, which, having emerged in the twenties of this century under the influence of R. Otto and his well known work, *The Idea of the Holy*, still continues its tradition today, basing itself rather on the idea of comprehension and participation and suggesting that the study of religion must begin at its true centre, that is, with 'religious experience'. The appeal to phenomenologico-hermeneutical criteria: to *Einfühlung* (identification) and *Verstehen* (understanding) has become a commonplace in this school, which, for that reason, prefers to talk, not of definition—as if religion was an object among other objects—but precisely of 'understanding', 'intuition' of and 'participation' in the religious world.

This particular sensitivity—to the religious—almost Eastern in character, one might say—requires one to trace the various components from which a definition/understanding of religion is gradually formed. Briefly, these are: (*a*) above all awareness that religion cannot be understood unless the starting point is 'religious experience', together with the presupposition that such an experience is meaningful for the man who lives through it; (*b*) emphasis on the argument according to which, if religion is 'religious experience', the student of religion must identify himself with the religious man. And taking this point still further, will one not then require that the researcher himself should be religious, in order to be able to understand, on the grounds that only within religious *Hörfeld* (earshot) is it possible to grasp religious meanings?; (*c*) the characterisation of religious experience in this school as the 'sense of the sacred'—which *vertical projection* of religious experience makes it possible for one to hold at arms length all forms of psychological, sociological, historicist and economic reductionism; (*d*) finally, the thesis that the sense of the sacred has its own real intentionality: it is a sentiment that corresponds to an authentic reality. In this last development, the definition/comprehension of religion is led to coincide with the truth of religion itself and as a result the science of religions turns into a theology of religions.[7]

In conclusion, the Marburg school is a religiously committed school which proposes an *intuitive, essential, ostensive* as well as *hermeneutico-theological* definition of religion, undertaking to bring the history of religion and theology of religion closer together, in the conviction that to understand the essence of religion is to participate in the truth of religion itself.

3. THE CHICAGO SCHOOL

The Chicago school can in some respects be regarded as a derivation of the Marburg school, not only ideally, on account of the hermeneutical programme it has evolved, but also historically, through the mediation of J. Wach, a follower of Weiler, who emigrated from Germany to America where he gave the first impetus to the study of the history of religions.

Today the undisputed leader of the Chicago school is M. Eliade, to whom I therefore refer in these notes.

It would be useless to look for a definition of religion in Eliade: religion has an identity of its own which is recognised intuitively and of which the structures are not functions of a particular culture, but rather the deep substrata of anthropology itself. The fundamental conception remains that of the Marburg school: the sacred as a primordial, authentic, irreducible experience, from which a comprehensive theory of *homo religiousus* must be reduced. At the beginning of the *Patterns in Comparative Religion* Eliade wrote: '. . . a religious phenomenon will emerge as such only on the condition that it is understood in its own mode of being, that is to say, studied according to religious criteria'.[8] Now, by creating this particular working space for religion, the Rumanian scholar does not merely have the negative intention of barring the way to all forms of reductionism; he also means to indicate positively the value of religion and of research into religions. An attempt at a positive definition of religion in relation to historico-positive research is made by Eliade in the preface of his last great work, *The History of Religious Ideas*. Here he writes: 'For the historian of religions every manifestation of the sacred is of consequence; every rite, every myth, every belief or divine image reflects the experience of the sacred and consequently implies the notions of *being, meaning* and *truth*'.[9]

If one wants to grasp the difference between the Marburg school and the Chicago school where the concept of religion is concerned, one will concentrate on the fact that the latter, in addition to having refined the hermeneutical criteria according to which it approaches the religious world, is more anthropological in character, in that it aims to graft the sacred and representations of the sacred onto the deeper reaches of human reality, and in addition makes use of a more morphological perspective, presenting a wide-ranging typology, at once descriptive and paradigmatic, of religious forms.

4. THE LANCASTER TREND

A recent trend, and one which I would say is still in formation as far as the method of studying religions is concerned, is that which was initiated in 1967 in the Department of Religious Studies in the University of Lancaster, under the aegis of Ninian Smart.

The concept of religion underlying this trend is distinguished by two fundamental features: first, in that it sees religion as a religious experience which touches man in the totality of his being, thus calling into play all the human sciences (poly-methodical approach) and reducing the importance of the history of religions in the study of religion; and second, in that this trend believes it can make use of an axiological definition of religion without at the same time being committed as far as the value of the truth of religion itself is concerned.[10] The distinction which should serve to keep the *science* of religion free from theological contaminations will appear all the more difficult, in that Smart, the leader of the school, introduces hermeneutical motifs into the understanding of religion, speaking of 'internal logic', of the need 'to take interior sentiments into account', and recognising that there is an intra-religious explanation that cannot be overlooked.

I would say that Smart's position, and that of the Lancaster scholars in general, is moving towards a 'religionist' understanding which is less historical than that of the other trends but more sensitive to the difficult constituency of the *science* of religion and theology.[11]

5. THE GRONINGEN GROUP

As one final trend in the attempt to define and understand religion, I think it is important to mention the *Groninger Arbeitsgemeinschaft zum Studium der Grundfragen und Methoden der Religionswissenschaft* whose aim is to make a comprehensive review of all the methodological problems of the science of religions. One of the most important publications of this group is *Religion, Culture and Methodology*, edited by T. P. Baaren and H. J. W. Drijvers, to which I refer briefly.[12] The Groningen group, more indebted to cultural anthropology than to the history of the religions, has reached substantial agreement in defining religion as 'a function of culture', bringing together elements from the definitions of religion of C. Geertz and E. Spiro. The definition in question has a sociological background, but it seeks not to reduce religion to its social element but rather to serve as a protest against 'theological absolutism'. It is stated in this context that in order to be in a position to speak of religion it is necessary that there should be a group of people with a *minimum* of institutionalisation and a *minimum* of ritual forms. Thus, through the observation of behaviour in the social context, the attempt is made to recover scientific objectivity in the study of religion.

In this trend, the attitude of anti-institutionism is natural—institutionism would have no place in a scientific discussion. Thus the *Verstehende Schule* would have an interesting aesthetic dimension, but no operational character, and would therefore be useless for the purposes of scientific research. The exclusion of every philosophical or religious presupposition should constitute the point of departure and the initial requirement for the seriousness of research.[13]

It can be said, however, that even this group is not so unified, and that Waardenburg—one of the greatest of the Groningen research scholars—pursues a quite different line, being concerned with the *meaning* of a religion within the culture, a meaning which cannot be an objective *datum*, but which is understood in the context of the ultimate meaning of life and constitutes emblematically 'the self-expression of human existence'.[14]

6. CONCLUSION

On the basis of the foregoing brief survey, I should like to make two concluding observations. The first is formal in character. If the problem of the definition of religion brings with it the problem of method or of methods of studying religion, one comes to realise that the problem of method is transformed into a problem concerning the epistemological *status* of the sciences in general and of the human sciences in particular, becoming thus a more radical problem and hence more difficult to solve.

My second observation is axiological. It is the intention of all the trends and schools outlined above to respect the autonomy and specificity of religion. Now in order to sustain confidence in this declared intention, should one not seek an 'autonomous' definition of religion in such a way that it would be possible to refer back to an original constant which might account for the autonomy of the religious world?

Thus it would seem that only in relation to such a constant is it possible to make other attempts to clarify the meaning of religion—attempts which will be able to modify but not compromise the original nucleus of identification and recognition of religion as religion.

Translated by Sarah Fawcett

Notes

1. I use the phrase 'history of religion' in the wide sense given it in America. For a precise terminological distinction see R. Pummer '*Religionswissenschaft* or Religiology?' *Numen* 19 (1972) especially 102-106.
2. On the difficulty of reaching a definition/understanding of religion, see R. Plummer'Recent Publications of the Methodology of the Science of Religion' *Numen* (1975) 168-182; D. Wiebe 'Is a Science of Religion Possible?' in *Studies in Religion* 7 (1978) 5-14; see too my own article 'Analisi critica di alcune recenti pubblicazioni' in *Teologia* 2 (1978) 164-188.
3. See U. Bianchi 'Storia delle religioni (oggetto e metodo)' in *Dizionario Teologico Interdisciplinario* (Turin 1977) III col. 31.
4. See U. Bianchi 'Recenti "Storie delle religioni" e altri studi sul tema', in *Rivista di storia e letteratura religiose* 14 (1978) 89.
5. *Ibid.*
6. See K. Rudolph 'Die "ideologikritische" Funktion der Religionswissenschaft' *Numen* 25 (1978) 17-39.
7. Pannenberg is moving in the same direction. See W. Pannenberg, 'Scienza della religione come ideologia della religione' *Epistemologia e teologia* (Brescia 1975) 338-350; see also C. N. Ratschow 'Methodik der Religionswissenschaft' in *Enzyklopädie der geisteswissenschaften Arbeitsmethoden* 9 (Munich-Vienna 1973) col. 347-400.
8. M. Eliade *Patterns of Comparative Religion* trs. R. Sheed (London 1971).
9. See M. Eliade *A History of Religious Ideas* trs. W. R. Trask (London 1979) I.
10. Smart writes: '. . . *the sense of the numinous is a fact, but the object it is supposed to reveal is not a fact.*' See N. Smart *The Science of Religion and the Sociology of Knowledge. Some Methodological Questions* (Princeton 1973) p. 63.
11. It may be necessary to recall that the expression 'science of religion' refers here to a very definite concept of 'science' that is not the one implied by *Religionswissenschaft*, which can easily be related to the humanistic context of *Geisteswissenschaft*.
12. T. Baaren and H. J. W. Drijvers eds. *Religion, Culture and Methodology* (Paris and The Hague 1973).
13. *Ibid.* 160, and *passim.*
14. *Ibid.* 166.

Lawrence Sullivan

History of Religions: The Shape of an Art

THE HISTORY of religions enjoys a time of productivity and hermeneutical quality unparalleled in the life of this young discipline.[1] It has moved beyond philological preoccupations with reconstructing reliable texts and beyond organising the enormous number of descriptions of religious rituals, songs, dances and arts. This first phase generated a debate, inherited by scholars in the field, over definition and origins of religion; a reaction to the discovery of the stunning cultural breadth and temporal depth of human history reported in the ethnographic and archaeological literature of the nineteenth century. In those first years, scholars of culture, who had pictured themselves working within a conceivable span of biblical time and within the comfortable spatial assumptions of the colonial period, found themselves trying to stand in a room without floor or walls. There was a rush to find a fixed point—a first premise either in a logical definition of religion or in an historicistic primordial origin—in a human history whose sweep suddenly had neither discoverable bottom nor discernible frontiers. Recovering from this intellectual and existential vertigo, the present scholars turn to interpreting meanings found in their religious documents. For the purposes of this volume, this essay passes over the important in-house methodological disputes of our field discussed in numerous concise articles.[2]

Due to what William James termed 'the power of fashion in things scientific', theology remains curiously immune to the excitement and insights of the general study of religions.[3] Introducing a new series of books addressed to fill this gap, Dario Zadra remarks: 'The rigidity of interpretative models is holding back an understanding that is ever more necessary, and that prevents the development of a process of cultural ecumenism necessary for the definition of common problems.'[4] Theology is most familiar with the historiography of religions of classical antiquity or those cultures of the Near East directly related to the Judaeo-Christian tradition.[5] But this decision to find interesting only cultures which have historicistic ties to the Judaeo-Christian tradition is arbitrary and limited in the extreme. The hermeneutic value of historicistic ties, in and of themselves, is not by any means clear: 'casual', chronological links do not automatically clarify the meanings of the symbols involved.

Hermeneuts of the history of religions are discovering that the sacred, though it takes various shapes in human history, is above all a magnificent achievement in the structure of human consciousness such that it is recognisable behind the different symbols of cultures far removed in time and space: in the great religious systems and small-scale societies of Asia, Oceania, Africa and the Americas. The spiritual creations which have grown up around sacred symbols are no mean human achievement. Recent scholarship makes the meaning of specific cultural creativities apparent and clear; but this religious experience, expressed in rite and symbol in the common province of human experience of the sacred, is not yet the stuff of theological reflection. I shall mention a few figures whose synthetic work gives the field its current orientation. In closing I shall touch upon areas of common interest to theology and history of religions; bridges between these two hermeneutical spheres. This notice is dangerously selective and neglects important areas. It is neither exhaustive, representative, nor a guide to orthodoxy in a field charactised by varieties of approach.

Many excellent scholars consider themselves to be 'historians of religions' because they accept exclusively historical methods and presuppositions. They are, in fact, however, experts in just one religion, and sometimes in the only one period or one aspect of that religion. . . . The historian of religions, in the broad sense of the term, cannot limit himself to a single area. He is bound by the very structure of his discipline to study at least a few other religions so as to be able to compare them and thereby understand the modalities of religious behaviours, institutions and ideas.[6]

Several important scholars, historians of religions *par excellence* in this synthetic sense, give the field its present texture: *Raffaele Pettazzoni, Henry Corbin, Ananda K. Coomaraswamy, Georges Dumézil, Mircea Eliade, and also Claude Lévi-Strauss whose impact on the study of religion is immense.*[7]

Raffaele Pettazzoni has left an indelible mark. The scope of his interpretative framework becomes a model in the field.[8] Beginning with historical studies of the religion of Sardinia and then Roman and Greek antiquity, he soon dedicated himself to the study of the whole history of religions. He investigated what Paul Radin has called 'the great and recurring, troubling themes of mankind': the mysteries, monotheism, the confession of sins, etc. A son of Croce's historicism, all his life he stressed the 'genomenon', or historicity, of every religious 'phenomenon'.[9] Nonetheless, he realised that 'religious phenomenology and history are not two sciences but are two complementary aspects of the integral science of religion, and the science of religion as such has a well-defined character given to it by its unique and proper subject matter'.[10]

Within this grand synthetic clearing in the study of religions have sprung up scholars, particularly in Italy, who write in the same comparative historical tradition, though their compass be of smaller scale. Among others G. Tucci, Uberto Pestalozza, Gillo Dorfles, Angelo Brelich, E. de Martino, V. Lanternari, Alessandro Bausani, Ugo Bianchi, Dario Sabbatucci, Maria G. Piccaluga. In an article on history of religions in Italy, Ioan P. Culianu presents some one hundred works in the history of religions published in the last four years.[11]

Henry Corbin is an example of the expansion of a mind by the material of his study. Beginning with European philosophy[12] he soon found sources of enrichment in scholars of Islamic philosophical traditions, especially Ismaelite and esoteric persuasion in Iran. As director of the Departement d'Iranologie de l'Institut Franco-Iranien in Teheran from 1946-1970 and Professor at the École des Hautes Etudes from 1954 on, Corbin's time was consumed by deciphering numbers of little known manuscripts. In spite of this, he pursued comparative studies in his important Eranos lectures delivered from 1949 to 1977. There he treated initiation, hermeticism in Iran, alchemy, cyclical time, notions of Celestial Earth and Spiritual body in Iranian traditions. The scope of his interests continued to enlarge; he studied gnosis, prophetology, medieval initiatory traditions, connections of Jewish theology and mysticism, etc. Corbin's text-critical responsibilities kept him from a comparative study of India, China, Japan, Tibet, archaic religions and folklore.

In 1974, four years before his death, Corbin, together with some thirty scholars mostly from France and Germany, founded a new type of university, the Centre International de Recherche Spirituelle Comparée in Cambrai, France. Dedicated to the research and practice of the ancient *chevalerie spirituelle* believed common to Christianity, Judaism and Islam, five volumes of lectures from their annual conferences have appeared under the heading *Cahier de l'Université Saint Jean de Jérusalem*.[13] Corbin concluded there are three sources of knowledge: (1) work of the intellect in philosophy; (2) the body of traditions in positive theology; (3) inner revelation of esoteric content in theosophy.[14]

Corbin's thrust is the inverse of Pettazzoni's: anti-historical,[15] philosophically inclined, limited to the religions 'of the Book', personally committed to a search for esoteric meaning of the Sacred Word which became the Holy Book, espousal of a gnostic and docetist bent of mind. Nonetheless, he gathered round him scholars who illumine our understanding of religions: Ernst Benz, Gilbert Durand, Antoine Faivre, Bernard Gorciex, Jean Servier, Richard Stauffer, and Jean-Louis Vieillard-Baron.

'There is no doubt that *Ananda Coomaraswamy* was one of the most learned and creative scholars of the century'[16] who represents still another facet of the field.[17] Like Pettazzoni and Corbin, he began his investigations in a single area: art and handicrafts in Indian history. This interest expanded through more profound understanding of hermeneutical method.[18] Thus he addressed general and comparative questions in the history of religions: ritual, mythology, cosmogony and chthonian fertility. Finally, he gave himself over to study 'the primordial and universal tradition present in every authentic nonacculturated civilisation':[19] the *philosophia perennis*. However, Coomaraswamy's approach did not reduce all religious manifestations to an abstract 'religious Esperanto', to use Lipsey's term, but 'rather he progressed by a comparative method, collating the formulae of one tradition with another, which kept in view the likelihood that all religions have a common source'.[20] Such first principles, no matter what we make of them, enabled him to interpret carefully and profoundly Indian art as well as religious expressions in pre-Aryan India, Vedism, Brahmanism, and Buddhism by integrating parallels from outside the Indian traditions. But briefly, he reveals new understandings about the nature of religious images, myth and symbol in general.

Georges Dumézil[21] combines historical and structural approaches to myth in an enormous comparative endeavour spanning all Indo-European religions. Due to the time invested in spunky defence of his early conclusions he has not elaborated a systematic theory of myth. Even so, scholars follow the direction of his thought and specialists utilise his conclusions in the field of mythology.

Under the influence of Marcel Mauss, Dumézil abandoned the sterile etymological intuitions of Max Müller for comparison of historically related socio-religious institutions, mythologies, and theologies of peoples of the same linguistic and cultural matrix. He elucidates an Indo-European conception of society comprised of three functions: sovereignty, war, and economy. To each function corresponds a socio-political category responsible for its execution (kings, warriors, food producers) and a type of divinity who presides over each sphere (in Rome, Jupiter, Mars, Quirinus). Dumézil's work illustrates how this system underwent reinterpretation in the separated histories of Indo-European peoples. Thus, he postulates that Roman mythologies place a peculiar importance on 'historical' people and events, as in the first book of *Histories* by Titus Livius, whereas in India this tripartite system was expressed in increasingly cosmological terms.

Dumézil sparks the interest of specialists who do not share his wide-ranging comparative abilities nor his interpretative over-view. More importantly, he is an example to historians of religions in his use of 'a meticulous philological and historical analysis of the texts with insights gained from sociology and philosophy. He has also shown that only by deciphering the basic ideological system underlying the social and religious institutions can a particular divine figure, myth, or ritual be correctly understood.[22]

Though not *sensu stricto* an historian of religions, *Claude Lévi-Strauss* has staggering impact on the discipline, on sciences of culture, and on the reading public.[23] He first applied to ethnography the models of phonology of Troubetzkoi and Jakobsen in which the structure of language exhibits a deep (i.e., unconscious) but perfectly logical coherence even though sounds, the surface features of language, seem only arbitrarily linked to the meanings they convey. By treating kinship, family relations, and social organisation as similar systems of communication, he demonstrates the rigorous logic undergirding all of what had been dubbed 'primitive' societies.[24] He concludes, as we must with him, 'that man has always been thinking equally well'.[25]

In like manner, in investigations of mythology, he does not look for the meaning of myth in conscious perception of its symbols but in the 'deep-structures', the logical relations between symbols. Myth attempts to overcome contradictions (e.g., life/death) or sets of them (earth/sky; nature/culture; inside/outside) through the play of logical combinations below the threshold of consciousness. Myth lies between and shares aspects of images (which are concrete) and concepts (which have power of reference). Because myth, unlike science, cannot extricate itself from concrete events and yet continues to refer to unconscious concepts (because it cannot help but be logical), it 'never tires of ordering and re-ordering in its search to find a meaning'.[26] It is bound to be both repeated and internally repetitious.

In a mammoth comparative study of American mythologies[27] his materials expand his evaluation of myth. A musical model is needed to supplement the phonetic one in order to enter the aesthetic, emotional and temporal[28] dimensions of myth. 'Music and mythology were, if I may say so, two sisters, begotten by language. . . . Music emphasises the sound aspect, mythology the meaning aspect embedded in language.'[29] Whatever one's verdict on the logico-linguistic nature of 'meaning'[30] and his ambitious materialist reductionism,[31] he forces scholars of culture, philosophers, literary critics and artists to dialogue with spiritual creations of mythic thought not long ago 'declared a disease of language, a naïve animism, a playful and debasing fancy, a projection of astral phenomenon, a verbalisation of ritual, or a fantasy related to a primordial parricide'.[32]

The *ouvre* of *Mircea Eliade*[33] is the prime moving force behind the history of religions.[34] Three characteristics contribute to its power: (*a*) coherence and singleness of purpose from beginning to end; (*b*) its didactic character aimed at fashioning a new discipline; (*c*) clarification of hermeneutic proper to the history of religions.[35] The interest of American universities and public in history of religions, where 'this discipline is better taught than in any other part of the world,'[36] is due to this scholar and his colleagues.

(*a*) Unless we keep in mind the unity of Eliade's whole scholarly work it overwhelms us with the diversity of the empirical data around which it takes shape: the religious beliefs, ideas and practices of human history. Eliade is a morphologist of the sacred who views his scholarship as scientific.[37] The study of religions demands exacting empirical investigation, accords first place to its data: social, mythic, dogmatic, musical, iconographic, liturgical. 'I would compare my immersion in the documents to a fusion with the material . . . drowned in the documents, what is personal, original, living, in me disappears, dies.'[38]

His task is empirical especially in the sense that the arrangement of data and procedures of investigation must be proper to the subject. The sacred should be examined in a light which allows one to recognise it as such. He chooses morphology as a suitable method.[39] His encounter with different concepts of history in Indian religion confirms this choice, for morphology arranges data in a logico-formal sequence which progresses from simple to complex; traces patterns of change without imposing unilinear chronology on order of their appearance. Reflection on concrete religious forms reveals a formal pattern which underlies them; reflection on the pattern reveals the creativity of their individual variations. Eliade discerns in each religious datum a formally simple 'centre': *hierophany*, the manifestation of the sacred in the mental world of those who believed in it.[40] Morphologically speaking, the sacred is an element in the structure of human consciousness and not a moment of human history. *Hierophany* has a recognisable structure: it reveals the nature and meaning of time, space, power and reality. It reveals a mode of being. In short, it is an appearance of, literally, 'Supreme Being'.

Hierophany is never found in this 'pure' elemental form[41] but in elaborated form; it grows and changes without becoming something else: profane. Thus the sacred appears in many different forms, 'animals, plants, gestures and so on . . . and as that has been going on for tens of thousands of years of religious life, it seems improbable that there remains anything that has not at some time been so transfigured'.[42]

Each form offers new revelations about sacred time, space, power and reality and reveals *different* modes of being while preserving the structure of *hierophany* (i.e., it is always true and real). Archaic religions are, therefore, presystematic ontologies. Eliade groups religious expression into patterns according to the formal similarities they exhibit: sky gods, earth gods, aquatic symbolism, etc.

Using such an approach, firstly, religion can be studied empirically as a *whole*, without overwhelming the scholar with its multiplicity of expression. Secondly, unlike Frazer's encyclopaedic collections which ignored differences between items, Eliade's approach welcomes the discovery of new creative expressions. Thirdly, it remains free of any single metaphysical definition of sacred which limits its application. Fourthly, such an empirical approach treasures the peculiar dimensions of the sacred which give religion its unique quality. It is a morphology of the sacred in a recognisably religious sense. For Eliade, then, the morphology of the sacred is at once a comparative method, a set of empirical descriptions of manifest forms, an epistemological quality in the structure of consciousness,[43] and a hermeneutical statement about the mode of human existence.

A 'theological' correlate is implied in his descriptions.[44] As the sacred manifests itself, it must, at the same time, withdraw and remain hidden. Eliade calls this the dialectic of the sacred. Religious expression is made possible by the retreat of the Supreme Being which no longer plays an active role in religious experience: the *deus otiosus*. When the Supreme Being becomes transcendent it is supplanted by other divine forms which are active, fertile, dramatic and so on. Then begins the history of religious man's movement toward the transcendent.

Eliade applies his morphology to different problems in the history of religions: initiation, alchemy, archaic techniques of ecstasy, the nature of symbols, myth, Australian religions, etc.[45] His *magnum opus*, *The History of Religious Ideas*, eliminates any doubt about the compatibility of morphology with the comparative historical approach of, say, Pettazzoni. It is a *tour de force* illustrating how a morphological grasp of data illumines both connections between symbols in separate cultures, where such links can be established, and highlights the uniqueness of any single historical expression. By lining up a series of all the variants their uniqueness falls into relief.

(*b*) The didactic character of Eliade's work is striking in certain major writings of general nature[46] which differ from those on specific problems. These didactic works are never the cutting edge of his research but reflective glances over his shoulder wherein he describes clearly for his audience tools he used to travel the distance he has come. Estimating it would take about 1,000 more hours to complete *From Primitives to Zen*, he wonders 'whether such a source book is worth all the trouble? . . . I've been living among these documents for about fifteen years'.[47] On the one hand, these works educate peer-scholars with whom Eliade wishes to dialogue but whose expertise lies outside the field of religion. On the other hand, they are service manuals which guide students through a labyrinth of materials and help younger scholars study religion as a whole. Eliade self-consciously tries to create a new discipline. The critical apparatus and annotated bibliographies of all his work reflects this. It would be a mistake to read them as 'evidence', 'proof', or 'examples' of his hypotheses. Instead, they are a service to those who dare immerse themselves in the data.

(c) The hermeneutical task of the historian of religions does not end with empirical morphology. One must enter into a union with the religious data—'relive' the multitude of existential situations—in order to understand both the plurality of modes of being and the singularity of the human condition expressed in them.[48] Historians of religions must produce, not erudite monographs, but *ouvres*[49] in the sense of alchemical spirituality: create works which at the same time transmute and create the worker. Since the sacred is a universal dimension whose correlative is man's specific existial situation, its interpretation, in this recreative sense, opens on to a new humanism. He ranges hermeneutics 'among the living sources of a culture'.[50] In the last account, Eliade sees hermeneutics as a vocation and a 'religious' experience: 'man's becoming aware of his own mode of being and assuming his *presence* in the world.'[51] By examining the *facts* of the religious universe Eliade evokes for modern man—helps him in fact to rediscover—the dimension of cosmic sacredness. Through his interpretations he revalorises the religiousness of human existence.

One need not share the assumptions of Eliade, Lévi-Strauss, Coomaraswamy, Dumézil, Corbin or Pattazzoni to bathe in the light they shed on humankind's religious life. Indeed they differ among themselves as do the scholars who bob in their wake. It would seem reasonable, on the face of it, that students of the various disciplines of theology would discover interesting material for reflection in the historico-religious interpretations of initiation, confession of sins, religious healing, symbolisms of water, fire, ritual, myth, prayer, priesthood and shamanism, divine-human figures, cosmology, God, angels, mysticism, religious ontology, city and rural religion, vegetation, fertility, divination and prophecy, creation, evil, sacred mysteries, death and after-life and a host of other areas which appear to be common to the two interpretative spheres of theology and history of religions.

More instructive than shopping for facile parallels in the history of religions is the lesson of these historians of religions: after thorough reflection on the great spirtual achievements in history, they bring back experiences from their documents much larger than their first questions could carry. The rich religious life of the breadth and depth of human history transmutes the categories of their queries. Whatever personal and communal decisions Judaeo-Christian theologians make concerning the unique character of their own tradition, their religious experience takes its place not only in a linear descent from Near Eastern, Classical Mediterranean or Indo-European cultures but side by side with contemporary and archaic manifestations of sacred totality, perfection, nostalgia, unity, divinity, transcendence and longing. These call for reflection.

Notes

1. J. Waardenburg 'Religionswissenschaft in Continental Europe' *Numen* 23 (1976) 219-237; U. Bianchi *The History of Religions* (Leiden 1975); D. Allen *Structure and Creativity in Religion* (The Hague 1978); G. Dudley *Religion on Trial* (Philadelphia 1977); L. M. Karpinski *The Religious Life of Man* (London 1978).

2. See M. Eliade 'History of Religions in Retrospect' in *The Quest* (Chicago 1977) pp. 12-36; J. Z. Smith *Map is not Territory* (Leiden 1977); U. Bianchi 'Storia delle religioni: oggetto e metodo' in the *Dizionario teologico interdisciplinario* (Milano 1977) V pp. 308-323.

3. Thus Urban T. Holmes 'What has Manchester to do with Jerusalem?' *Sewanee Rev,* (1976).

4. D. Zadra *Le scienze umane* (Milano 1977) I p. 95.

Some interest is shown in Asian, Islamic philosophy and ethics *qua* systems.

6. M. Eliade *The Quest* p. 78.

7. Regrettably left aside are figures of the stature of Joachim Wach, Gerardus van der Leeuw, Wilhelm Schmidt, Louis Massignon, etc.

8. See the bibliography of his work in M. Gandini *Studi e Materiali di Storia delle Religione* 31 (1961) 3-31.

9. Pettazzoni *La Religion dans la Grèce antique* (1953) pp. 18-19.

10. Pettazzoni in *The History of Religions* (1959) p. 66.

11. 'History of Religion in Italy: the State of the Art' in *History of Religions* (in press).

12. M. Eliade 'Some Notes on Theosophia Perennis' in *History of Religions* 19 No. 2. 167-176; for a bibliography of Henry Corbin see *Mélanges offerts a Henry Corbin* (Teheran 1977) nos. 20, 23, 28, 61.

13. 1, *Sciences traditionelles et sciences profanes* (1974); 2, *Jerusalen la Cité spirituelle* (1975); 3, *La Foi prophetique et le sacre* (1976); 4, *Les Pelerins de l'Orient et les vagabonds de l'occident* (1977); 5, *Les Yeux de chair et les yeux de Feu* (1979) (Paris).

14. *Cahiers de l'Université Saint Jean de Jérusalem* 1, 35.

15. Stemming from his conviction that 'la chevalerie spirituelle n'était pas uniquement . . . une comtemplation fervente du passé . . . (mais) le sentiment d'appartenir à une même famille spirituelle, d'avoir en commun la même vision' *Cahiers* 5, 12.

16. M. Eliade 'Some notes . . .' cited in Note 12, at p. 171.

17. See Schuyler Camman 'Remembering Again' *Parabola* 3 No. 2 84-91.

18. See *Coomaraswamy* I ed. Roger Lipsey: *Selected Papers: Traditional Art and Symbolism* II: *Metaphysics* III: *His Life and Work* (Princeton 1977).

19. M. Eliade 'Some Notes . . .' cited in Note 12, at p. 169.

20. Lipsey 3 277; Eliade 'Some Notes . . .' p. 170.

21. For a bibliography of Dumézil see C. Scott Littleton *The New Comparative Mythology* (Revised Edition) (Berkeley 1973) pp. 242-246.

22. M. Eliade *The Quest* p. 34.

23. See F. H. and C. C. Lapointe *Claude Lévi-Strauss: An International Bibliography* (New York 1977).

24. Lévi-Strauss *Les Structures élémentaires de la parenté* (Paris 1949); *Anthropologie structurale* (Paris 1958); *Le Totémisme aujord'hui* (Paris 1962).

25. Lévi-Strauss 'Structural Study of Myth' in *Myth: A Symposium* ed. T. Sebeok p. 66.

26. Lévi Strauss *The Savage Mind* (Chicago 1966) p. 22.

27. Lévi-Strauss *Introduction to a Science of Mythology* (three volumes published) (New York).

28. 'It is as if a diachronic set of events was simultaneously projected on the screen of the present' *Myth and Meaning* (New York 1977) p. 38.

29. Lévi-Strauss *Myth and Meaning* pp. 53-54.

30. 'To speak of rules and to speak of meaning is the same thing' *Myth and Meaning* p. 1.

31. He believes local structure inheres in the very structure of matter.

32. Eliade 'Myth' *Dictionary of the History of Idea* III (1973) p. 317.

33. See bibliography in C. Tacou *Mircea Eliade* (Paris 1978) pp. 391-409.

34. See G. Dudley cited in note 1: J. A. Saliba *Homo Religiosus in Mircea Eliade* (Leiden 1976); D. Allen *Structure and Creativity in Religion* (The Hague 1978).

35. See Tacou, pp. 11-15, for brief biography and intellectual history of Eliade.

36. Eliade *No Souvenirs* (New York 1977) p. xiv.

37. See Tacou for Eliade's work in entomology, botany, mineralogy as well as *No Souvenirs*, pp. 4, 98 and 254.
38. Eliade *No Souvenirs* p. 92
39. Goethe initiated morphological studies with *Morphology of Plants*. Eliade's affinity with him would occupy a book. 'The mystery of this *total* attraction with Goethe still fascinates me'; Eliade *No Souvenirs* p. 316.
40. Eliade *Patterns in Comparative Religions*, Chapter One.
41. *Ibid.* p. 30.
42. Eliade *Patterns* p. 12.
43. See P. Ricoeur 'Le symbole donne à penser' *Esprit* (July-August 1959).
44. Eliade *Patterns* pp. 38-123; *Sacred and Profane* esp. pp. 118-128.
45. *Rites and Symbols of Initiation* (New York 1958); *The Forge and the Crucible* (Chicago 1978); *Shamanism* (Princeton 1964); *Images and Symbols* (1969); *Zalmoxis, The Vanishing God* (Chicago 1978); *Australian Religions* (Ithaca 1973).
46. Notably in *Patterns in Comparative Religions, The Sacred and the Profane, Myth and Reality, The Quest* and *From Primitives to Zen*.
47. Eliade *No Souvenirs* p. 218.
48. Eliade *The Quest* p. 10.
49. Eliade *ibid.* p. 61.
50. *Ibid.* p. 61.
51. Eliade *The Quest* p. 9.

Contributors

JACQUES AUDINET was born in 1928 and studied both in Paris and in Chicago. He teaches at the Institut Catholique, at the Institut Supérieur de Pastorale Catéchétique and in the Faculte de Théologie in Paris, and he has also been visiting professor at Fordham University, the University of San Francisco, and the Mexican American Cultural Center in San Antonio, Texas. He was director of the Institut Supérieur de Pastorale Catéchétique between 1969 and 1976, and he has published many books and articles on religious pedagogy and practical theology.

GREGORY BAUM was born in 1923 in Berlin. He has lived in Canada since 1940 and was ordained to the priesthood in 1954. He is professor of theology and sociology at St Michael's College in the University of Toronto. He is editor of *The Ecumenist* and co-editor of the *Journal of Ecumenical Studies*. His books include *Man Becoming* (1970), *New Horizon* (1972) and *Religion and Alienation* (1975).

JOHN B. COBB is professor of theology at the Claremont School of Theology and of religion at the Claremont Graduate School. He is also director of the Center for Process Studies and publisher of the journal *Process Studies*. His recent publications include *Christ in a Pluralistic Age* (1975) and *Theology and Pastoral Care* (1977). With David Griffin he wrote *Process Theology: An Introductory Exposition* (1976).

SEGUNDO GALILEA was born in Santiago de Chile in 1928 and ordained in 1956. Since 1963 he has worked with CELAM and the Conference of Religious in Latin America, organising pastoral and spiritual conferences throughout the continent. His published works include several articles for *Concilium* and other reviews, and books on evangelisation, pastoral strategy, popular religion and the way to follow Christ in Latin America.

PAUL KNITTER is professor of theology at Xavier University, Cincinnati. He studied theology at the Gregorian University, Rome, and the University of Marburg, West Germany. He has published *Towards a Protestant Theology of Religions* (1974) and various articles dealing with the dialogue between Christianity and World Religions.

MATTHEW LAMB studied at the Gregorian University in Rome and at the State University of Münster, West Germany, under the direction of Prof. Johann B. Metz (Dr.Theol.). He is a diocesan priest, associate professor of fundamental theology at Marquette University, Milwaukee, Wisconsin, and visiting associate professor of fundamental theology at the Divinity School, University of Chicago. Among his publications are studies on Bernard Lonergan's method, W. Dilthey's critique of historical reason, critical theory, political and liberation theologies, socio-economics and theology, and the relationship between theory and praxis.

ITALO MANCINI was born in Urbino in 1925. He studied at the Catholic University of Milan and became a priest in the diocese of Urbino. He teaches theoretical philosophy in the free university of Urbino. He is also director of the Instituto Superiore di Scienze Religiose at this university and president of the Teilhard de Chardin Institute. His principal works on the philosophy of religion are: *Filosofia della religione* 2nd ed. (Rome 1978); *Teologia ideologia utopia* 2nd ed. (Brescia 1978); *Novecento teologico* (Florence 1977); *Con quale cristianesimo* 2nd ed. (Rome 1979).

MARTIN MARTY was born in 1928 at West Point, Nebraska. He was ordained to the Lutheran Ministry. He is the Fairfax M. Cone Distinguished Service Professor at the University of Chicago, where he earned his Ph.D. in 1956. He has taught the history of modern Christianity (since 1963) in the Divinity School, the Committee on the History of Culture, and as an associate in the Department of History. Dr Marty is also associate editor of *The Christian Century,* editor of the newsletter *Context* and co-editor of *Church History.* The author of numerous books, including the recent *A Nation of Behavers* and *Religion, Awakening and Revolution*, he won the National Book Award in 1972 for *Righteous Empire*. Marty has contributed to the major international encyclopedias and written many journal articles. His current project, *Sacred Journeys,* is an illustrated work on 500 years of American religion and a possible television series based on it.

MALCOLM J. McVEIGH was born in Painesville, Ohio in 1931. He studied theology at Drew Theological Seminary and at the University of Heidelberg. After that he served as a Methodist missionary in Angola, Africa, and later worked for the Congo Protestant Relief Agency in Kinshasa, Congo (now Zaire). From 1971 to 1976 he taught in the Department of Philosophy and Religious Studies at the University of Nairobi and was also involved in religious research. Since June 1978 he has been pastor of the United Methodist Church in Sussex, New Jersey. He has served as an editor of the *Kenya Churches Handbook: The Development of Kenyan Christianity 1498-1973*, and his Ph.D. dissertation was published in 1974 under the title *God in Africa: Conceptions of God in African Traditional Religion and Christianity.*

LAWRENCE E. SULLIVAN was born in Boston, Massachusetts in 1949. He holds a B.A. degree in theology from St Francis College in Milwaukee, Wisconsin, the M.Divinity degree from Catholic Theological Union, Chicago, Illinois and the M.A. in history of religions from the University of Chicago. He has taught and carried out research as well as pastoral work in Zaire, Mexico, Italy and Belgium. He is now at the University of Chicago from which he holds the Ph.D.(cand.) in history of religions.

ALDO NATALE TERRIN was born at Fosso (Venezia) in 1942 and was ordained to the priesthood in 1965. After gaining degrees in philosophy and theology at Milan, he completed his studies at the Indologisches Seminar of the University of Münster, where, for five semesters, he followed courses in Sanskrit and eastern philosophy. At present he conducts the seminar in eastern philosophy at the Catholic University in Milan, and is a lecturer in the science of religions at the Institute for Pastoral Liturgy of St Justina in Padua (affiliated with S. Anselmo in Rome). His publications include *Scienza delle religioni e teologia nel pensiero di Rudolf Otto* (Brescia 1978) and a number of articles on the methodology of the science of the religions. He has edited the Italian edition of *Le cinque grandi religioni del mondo* (Brescia 1977) and recently he published a number of essays on the contribution of the science of religions to the understanding of popular religiosity—AA. VV. *Le religiosità popolare. Cammino di liberazione* (Bologna 1978); AA. VV. *La religiosità popolare nella Bibbia, nella liturgia, nella pastorale* (Bologna 1979).

VICTOR TURNER was born in Glasgow, Scotland, in 1920. After having studied and taught anthropology in England, he came to teach it at Cornell University, and is now professor of anthropology and religious studies in the University of Virginia. His books include the following: *The Ritual Process: Structure and Anti-Structure* (1969); *The Forest of Symbols* (1967); *Dramas, Fields and Metaphors* (1974); *Revelation and Divination in Ndembu Ritual* (1975); *Image and Pilgrimage in Christian Culture* (1977).

LIBRARY OF DAVIDSON COLLEGE

Books on regular loan may be checked out for **two weeks**. Books must be presented at the Circulation Desk in order to be renewed.

A fine is charged after date due.

Special books are subject to special regulations at the discretion of the library staff.

JAN 31 1985

DEC 15 '90